WRITING
CRIME
FICTION

Books in the 'Writing' series

Freelance Writing for Newspapers *by* Jill Dick

Writing for Children *by* Margaret Clark

Writing Crime Fiction *by* H.R.F. Keating

Writing Historical Fiction *by* Rhona Martin

Writing for Magazines *by* Jill Dick

Writing a Play *by* Steve Gooch

Writing Popular Fiction *by* Rona Randall

Writing for Radio *by* Rosemary Horstmann

Writing for the Teenage Market *by* Ann de Gale

Writing for Television *by* Gerald Kelsey

Writing a Thriller *by* André Jute

Writing about Travel *by* Morag Campbell

Other books for writers

Writers' & Artists' Yearbook

Word Power: a guide to creative writing *by* Julian Birkett

Research for Writers *by* Ann Hoffmann

WRITING CRIME FICTION

Second Edition

H R F Keating

A & C Black · London

Second edition 1994
First edition 1986
A & C Black (Publishers) Limited
35 Bedford Row, London WC1R 4JH

© 1994, 1986 H.R.F. Keating

ISBN 0–7136–3921–0

A CIP catalogue record for this book is available
from the British Library

The illustration on the front cover is by
Alan Forster

Typeset in 11/12 pt Palatino by Florencetype Ltd,
Kewstoke, Avon
Printed in Great Britain by Biddles Ltd, Guildford,
Surrey

Contents

	Preface for the Second Edition	vii
	Introduction	1
1	The Classical Blueprint	4
2	The Modern Variations	25
3	Transatlantic Cousins and Others	43
4	On the Periphery	59
5	How to Begin, Go On and Finish	85
6	Last Words	105
	Books Recommended	109
	Index	111

Preface for the Second Edition

I wrote this little book in 1986. Now in 1994 the opportunity
has arisen for a new, revised edition. Revised? So was what
I said back then wrong? I am happy to say that, reading over
the book again, I haven't felt the need to alter anything except
to take into account changes that have happened in the inter-
vening years. So some of the nitty-gritty advice about publishers and publishing has needed updating, and here and
there I have found newer and more easily accessible examples
of the various kinds of crime writing I speak about, and once
or twice I have put in new nuggets of the wisdom of others
gathered in my reading over the past eight years.

But during those years one factor has, indeed, altered the
way I have thought about the book. Now its image in my
mind has been enhanced by the reception that first edition
has had. First, from the kind words of some of my established
colleagues, in reviews and elsewhere. Ruth Rendell called it
'enormously entertaining' at least as readable as many of the
crime novels it cites. P. D. James, when we were co-tutors at
an Arvon Foundation course, gave it her imprimatur.
Margaret Yorke used the word 'magisterial' and added that
even experienced writers might pick up useful tips. That
delightful writer, Joan Aiken, told me she still consults it from
time to time.

But more pleasing to me even than those comments have
been the letters of appreciation I have had over the years from
would-be writers of crime fiction in Britain and from those
reading the American edition. On one occasion at least a
writer acknowledged gaining publication from following the
advice I gave, after her book had been rejected earlier.

So let me conclude this preface by repeating one piece of
advice I hope that author found of benefit, which I feel comes
better here than where it was in the first edition. I beg you,
I said then, to read all the book, however little any particular

subject seems relevant to your aspirations. In almost every chapter and section I have found it convenient to say things about crime writing in general and sometimes the art of fiction in particular.

I hope that among the new readers this edition may have there will be more than one who will find its pages as helpful as did the writers of all the letters I received. The best of good luck (because that you will need too) to you all.

H.R.F. Keating

Introduction

What is crime fiction, the kind of writing that you, who have taken up this book, are contemplating bringing into existence? It is a branch of literature that is by no means easy to define, for all that publishers happily put the label 'Crime' on a considerable proportion of their fiction output, for all that librarians regularly set aside enticing shelves with that same label.

The best I can do by way of pinning down a many-headed monster is to say that it is fiction that is written primarily for its entertainment value which has as its subject some form of crime. Crime writing is fiction that puts the reader first, not its writer. Pure novels are written because their authors believe or feel that they have something to say. Crime writers have to take a decision that, even though they may feel they have something to say, they will subordinate the saying of it where necessary to the simple task of keeping their readers' noses stuck in the pages.

That may make crime fiction sound like the merest journeyman work, but providing thoroughly absorbing entertainment in this world, which has been called not without justice a vale of tears, is no mean calling. The writer of crime fiction can feel he or she is doing a job worth doing.

Crime fiction is entertainment fiction. But why should that entertainment take the form of writing about crime? About evil?

Only because crime and evil exist. You can, if you are that way inclined, see all human life in terms of the opposition between Evil and Good. And the evil is perhaps the more fascinating. It arises both from within our nature and from the way we as human beings are bound to live closely linked one with another, whether we like it or not.

All of us, to a greater or lesser extent, do not like it. If we live in a society we have to live according to some rules. We have to drive on the left. Or on the right. But what we would like to do, were we free, is to drive down the middle of the broad highway. We would, if we could, break the laws that we know we need.

But from the earliest times there have been surrogate law-breakers. There have been people, freed from the complications of existing in the real world, who have been able to break the rules. These have been the creatures of fiction, created by the storyteller crouched by the hearth or sitting cross-legged under the palm-tree.

These tales of men and women who defied the rules and conventions were the earliest crime fiction. The strain has gone on ever since. When, with the advent of cheap printing, the stories ceased to be passed by word of mouth we had the beginnings of what the literary historians have called Sensational Literature. Dr Watson tells us in his earliest writings that Sherlock Holmes' knowledge of it was 'immense'.

But almost as soon as these stories about those who dared to break the laws came to be told, the listeners at the fireside or in the palm-tree's shade must have felt the need for their exact opposite. The lawbreaker is a dangerous fellow, a threat to peaceful existence. So what is needed to counterbalance him is the upholder of the law, the detective, though it was to be hundreds and thousands of years before any such recognisable law officer was to be found.

So crime fiction came into being, flourished and still continues, thank goodness, to flourish. Readers want it, in all or some of its many forms. A story, Damon Runyon said once, had better have 'some larceny in it because it is only human nature to be deeply interested in larceny. And readers want to know, too, what they are getting.' So the publishers are right to put that label 'Crime' on such of their products that they see as catering to that want. The librarians are right to set aside those shelves.

Crime writers, in fact, put their seal to a special contract with crime readers. It is nothing signed. There is no 'party of the first part' and 'whereas and wherefore' about it. It is invisible. But it exists. It exists in the form perhaps of the word 'Death' in a book's title, or 'Inspector'; in the particular colour of a paperback or in the jacket illustration of a hard-back. And what it says is, 'I, the writer, pledge myself to put you, the reader, first. I will entertain you, and I will entertain you with a story of crime, whether extolling a breaker of rules or extolling the upholder of them.'

What it does not say, or says only in the smallest of print in pale grey ink, is, 'I may also slip you a Mickey Finn by way of telling you something about this world you live in'. Because the crime story can, to a small extent or to quite a large extent, do what the pure novel does. It can make a temporary map for its readers out of the chaos of their sur-roundings. Only it should never let them know.

1
The Classical Blueprint

Let's start with the classical detective story, sometimes called the old-fashioned detective story. And indeed it is old-fashioned. Its heyday was round about 1930 and not all that many pure examples of it are being published today, though there are enough to make it a possible type of book to write if you are strongly inclined this way. But the reason I begin with it is because it is in many ways a blueprint.

Most of the other forms of crime fiction spring from it, either in angry reaction or attempted improvement. A lot of what it has in it is also to be found in all sorts of other books in the genre. Even a writer as far removed from the field covered in this book as John Le Carré owed a great deal in his earlier work, to the blueprint detective story. So even if it makes no particular appeal to you, read I beg you, this chapter.

First then, what exactly is the simple detective story, to use the term it was known by in that 1930s heyday? P. D. James, one of the best writers who out of love for the old detective story has taken it and made something more of it, once summed it up very neatly. There is, she says, always a mysterious death at its heart. There is always a closed circle of suspects (so there can be no question of someone unconnected with the setting coming in from outside and doing the deed, as might well happen in 'real life') and each of these suspects has to have a credible motive as well as reasonable opportunity of committing the crime and reasonable access to the means with which it was committed. Then the central character has to be the detective who eventually must solve the mystery. And finally the detective must uncover the murderer by logical deduction from facts fairly put before the reader.

Let us take each of these musts in turn. First, must it be murder? Well, yes, though there is no absolutely logical reason why, and indeed the book that was called by the poet T. S. Eliot, 'the first, longest and best' classical detective story,

Wilkie Collins' *The Moonstone* (Read it if you haven't done so.) managed very well with no more than the theft of a diamond. But, this exception proving the rule, notice that the diamond in question was an enormously valuable, unique jewel. In other words, it was important. And the reason murder is a virtual necessity in the detective story is that, in an essentially frivolous sort of book, it gives the reader a paradoxical feeling that here is something worth reading about.

It gives readers that necessary tug which will take them through all sorts of possibly wearisome matters to the final page. All along, as far as possible, they ought to be asking themselves that marvellously gripping, simple question 'Who did it?'

Suspects

A closed circle of suspects. Two good reasons for this. First, what you might call a local bye-law; a rule for this particular sort of book. There must be 'fair play' as between writer and reader. That may sound silly, but readers of blueprint detective stories want pure detection. They want a puzzle to solve. I do not believe, though many readers are convinced of it, that this is what finally attracts them, otherwise they might just as well do a crossword puzzle. But it is important all the same to provide the game as well as the story. Hence fair play, one of the rules of which is that the eventual murderer shall be one of a small group, delimited in some way.

The second reason for having a small circle of suspects is purely technical. It is extremely hard to write about even a dozen different people within a relatively short span. (Publishers will look askance at a straightforward detective story much over 80 000 words). It is hard to portray them so that your readers will know who is who each time one of them appears. And if you are to provide them with decent motives for a murder, and decently different ones as well, you will need room to do it in.

As to how you close the circle. Well, there are many different ways. You don't have to have the country house surrounded by untrodden snow, though you could still have that or some similar strictly physical limitation. After all, it is the readers who want to have this closed circle, and most of them are happy to suspend disbelief a little to get it. But a more likely way of achieving this basic necessity is to write something like

'Only a person who knew that Aubrey St John was going to be here at this time could have killed him'. If you put such a statement firmly into the mouth of your detective or state it flatly yourself, the reader will realise, even without consciously doing so, that this is the limit set for the game, the frame of the crossword puzzle, and will plunge on happily.

Each suspect must have a credible motive. Here again your reader, wanting to read the sort of book you are writing, will be prepared to give you a certain amount of latitude. In real life it is really not very likely that six people (and six is about the right number, pushing upwards to eight and down to a minimum of three, though you have to be skilled to have that few) will each have good reason for committing the same murder. But in the somewhat artificial world you are creating, six different motives you may well need.

So what should they be? Well, Edgar Wallace (a writer not to be despised, as he sometimes is) once said that vanity is at the back of most murders, and he had as a reporter covered many a murder trail. The notorious Dr Crippen, he pointed out, in fact murdered his assertive wife only because he was too vain simply to run away from her and make himself a target for scorn. So look at your friends, see what they are a little vain about and then multiply by a factor of ten.

Or, to get at it another way, here is a miscellaneous list from my own notebook of possible motives for murder:

- financial gain,
- self-protection,
- to preserve status,
- fear,
- to protect a loved one,
- for a principle,
- for revenge (but remember credibility here: only in some societies is revenge stoked up enough to lead to killing),
- the drive to power,
- compensation for past humiliation,
- removing a bar to sexual happiness (bother the permissive society, but impediments do still exist),
- jealousy,
- the desire to cock a giant snook at the entire world.

Human attributes these, that can fuel the mightiest of tragedies. But they can also be used to play the game that is the simple blueprint detective story. And they, of course, fuel the form of crime fiction that attempts to do something more than indulge in a contest with the reader—the books I call the detective novel and the crime novel.

So, if you have decided that the basic form is what suits your talents best (and, as I have said, books like this are still published), then you will find you need to use as your suspects what are often called cardboard characters, that is, people observed almost entirely from the outside and generally endowed with just one outstanding trait. (You are in a good tradition here, though; the 'humours' of Ben Jonson's classic plays are cardboard characters, if endowed with tremendous vitality.) Only your detective, perhaps, will need to be seen in somewhat greater depth, since your readers have got to sympathise with him or her and to do that they probably need more than just one point of contact.

Finally, here is a useful formula for establishing your circle of suspects. I take it from a detective story of the 1930s written by J. C. Masterman, a World War II spymaster and later Vice-Chancellor of Oxford University. He has his sleuth say once that to commit a murder you need four aces, Spades (the opportunity), Hearts (a motive), Diamonds (the capability of killing), and Clubs (the capability of committing this particular crime). Applying this little gimmick to each of your potential suspects, as I have once or twice found helpful, will prepare you to deal with P. D. James's next two necessary points: reasonable opportunity of committing the crime and reasonable access to the means with which it was committed.

The detective

The first thing to say about the detective, him or her, is that he or she need not be a professional. Of course, if you have even a distant eye on a whole series of books featuring one detective (and the late Margery Allingham once pointed out to me that the advantage of this is that half your potential readers want to read you and half want to read about your sleuth), then you are likely to land in difficulties if you hit on, say, a Victorian governess who happens to deal in the course of her scholastic career with as many as twenty or thirty 'orrible murders. I speak from embarrassed experience, having once embarked under the nom-de-plume of Evelyn Hervey on just such a foolish enterprise.

However, there are advantages to having an amateur detective of some sort, for you do not need to learn much about actual police procedures. You can concentrate the detecting on to one single personality, and thus concentrate your reader's attention equally. You can write about the sort of person you know well, or even are.

In my first book, *Death and the Visiting Firemen*, back in 1959, I made my detective a schoolmaster (as my father had been) and was able to use a teacher's summing-up of a class of twenty or thirty potential delinquents as a parallel for an investigator's examining of six or so suspects. And, when you think of it, many professions require a similar ability. It is certainly applicable to certain niches in society, as witness that archetypal gossipy spinster, Agatha Christie's Miss Marple, whose love of knowing everything about everybody made her quite plausibly a solver of crimes, if not of quite as many murders as eventually came her way.

Miss Marple is, in fact (quiet-mannered village pussy though she was), an example of nothing less than the Great Detective. And it is worth taking a little time to look at this personage. He or she is not nowadays very likely to feature in the book you may write, but the idea lies at the heart of detective fiction and still exercises a subtle influence.

The Great Detective, then, was an investigator possessed of powers beyond those of the ordinary mortal. Edgar Allan Poe's Chevalier Auguste Dupin was the first of the breed. Sherlock Holmes is the prime example. You may, looking back at the stories about those two (and you should have read them, twice over) think they are no more than high old eccentrics bright enough to solve intriguing cases. You would be wrong. The Great Detective is a figure of myth, something more than he seems, an example to the world. That is why you will still see caricatures of Sherlock Holmes in newspaper cartoons and advertisements, and that, too, is why the Great Detective, although unlikely to be a creation of your own, is worth some consideration.

Great Detectives, for all that they appear in mere detective stories, are figures to parallel with the great poet and the great scientist because in solving the sort of genuinely baffling mystery that confronts them, in fact they go some way to solving a yet greater mystery, the mystery of the human personality. The Great Detective is a person endowed with the power of entering into the minds of others. (Remember Dupin being able to tell his friend step by step just what his silent train of thought had been, and Holmes doing the same to Watson.) The Great Detective is, then, a liberating figure, not locked as most of us are in the prisons (or locked rooms) of our own preconceived ideas. It is when Great Detectives make a jump out of such ideas that they solve the baffling mystery, that they see, to quote a famous example from Poe, that the best place to hide a letter is in a letter-rack. They produce the genuinely startling solution out of a tranced (generally tobacco smoke wreathed) combination of the intuitive and the rational.

Alas, it is not given to most of us to be the sort of genius Edgar Allan Poe was (most of the time), or even to be able to walk in his footsteps like Conan Doyle, G. K. Chesterton, Dorothy L. Sayers and Agatha Christie, with those steps getting fainter and fainter along the way.

We lesser mortals have to be content with the Lesser Detective. But he or she must still be some sort of a hero. The crime has got to be solved by your detective, not by a piece of luck. Not by someone else stepping in at the last moment. The reader has identified with the person you have put at the centre of your story and that person must, for the reader's satisfaction, bring off the final solution.

Yet such a figure need not be too heroic. Indeed, the more heroic you make your hero the more you will need moments of human weakness to make it easy for readers to have that sympathetic identification. Remember Sherlock Holmes' impatience and his touches of vanity. Your hero can even be, like my Inspector Ghote of the Bombay C.I.D., a figure who appears not to be a hero. But if you set out on that rather tricky path, you will find before you finish that you have subtly to make this unheroic figure a hero after all. He must in the end get his man, and do it in a way the reader will find credible.

Inspector Ghote, I once remarked a little pretentiously to an interviewer, c'est moi. Whatever figure you choose as a hero, you will hardly be able to keep out something of yourself. And it is no bad idea to choose someone not too distant from oneself, especially if you hope to create a detective capable of standing up to a whole series of books. If your hero or heroine is too much of a concocted stereotype, you may find yourself bitterly regretting the iron limits you have confined him or her in. Of course, you can change the fellow, as for instance Margery Allingham did over a good many years with her Mr Campion, who started out as a form of imitation Scarlet Pimpernel and ended as an acute and compassionate observer of human follies. Dorothy L. Sayers' Lord Peter Wimsey went through a fairly similar transfiguration.

The Watson

A word here about that frequently-found adjunct of the Great Detective, the Watson. Curiously enough the character generally labelled in this way was not the discovery of Conan Doyle; was not John Watson M.D. tagging faithfully along behind Sherlock Holmes. The figure originates with the originator of the whole genre of detection, Edgar Allan Poe. In three short stories about Le Chevalier Dupin, *The Murders in the Rue Morgue, The Mystery of Marie Roget* and *The Purloined Letter*, Poe laid down virtually all the essentials of the genre which continues happily to this day. In recounting his hero's feats of ratiocination (a word he invented) he had an anonymous, somewhat credulous, narrator following him everywhere and asking the sort of questions the reasonably intelligent reader might want to ask; the original Watson.

The device is tremendously useful. It enables you as the writer to tell the reader just as much of what your detective is thinking as you want to. The moment when it enters his or her head, that X was the one who did it, can thus be concealed and brought out only at the very end of the story.

You can give your reader all the clues which, in the name of fair play, you are bound to do without explaining anything of their significance.

> Watson: Is there any other point to which you would wish to draw my attention?
> Holmes: To the curious incident of the dog in the night-time.
> Watson: The dog did nothing in the night-time.
> Holmes: That was the curious incident.

No need to say more. Watson wonders, and the reader, if bright enough, works out that if a dog does not bark when an intruder comes to commit a crime, then the crime is an inside job. Your Watson, then, needs to be just a little less intelligent than you conceive your readers as being. But only a little. Remember the reader steps into the Watson's shoes.

Yet he is not an absolutely necessary member of your cast of characters. A murderer you must have, and a victim or victims. A detective you must have, and suspects to be investigated and one by one to be thought of by your reader as the guilty party. But you can tell this sort of story without the detective having a particular friend in whom they confide.

You can instead tell your tale from what I call the 'angel over the shoulder' point of view. That is, you write as if you were positioned just behind and above your detective. You tell the reader everything your sleuth sees and hears (fair play) and you have the ability partly to enter the detective's head when and where you want to. You can do this to the extent of saying as Agatha Christie (who abandoned Hercule Poirot's charmingly bumbling Captain Hastings quite early) does in *One, Two, Buckle my Shoe*: 'For the first time Hercule Poirot was looking at the case the right way up.' The more conscientious among her readers would at these words stop and think, knowing that they too could, if they were clever enough, look at it all in the right way.

Clues

This brings us to the final ingredient in P. D. James' recipe. The detective must uncover the murderer by logical deduction from facts fairly put. No inspired guesses, though your hero may 'suddenly' see the logic of the situation. But the means of deduction must be there for your reader to go through alongside your detective. So what about the facts fairly put? They are quite simply your clues. Then where are these limits of fairness? Certainly you are obliged in this game you have undertaken to play against the reader (while at the same time telling a good story) to state the physical circumstances necessary to unmasking the murderer. But there is more than one way of stating.

Dorothy L. Sayers once said, in her blunt way, that any fool can tell a lie, but that the clever detective-story writer will tell the truth in such a way that the readers are seduced into telling the lie for themselves. Look at the way how in *The Nine Tailors* she puts before you the truth about the devastating sound of church bells ringing and induces you to tell yourself the lie that the description is there only for its own sake.

Perhaps the best way of tricking readers into seeing but not seeing what you put in front of them is by stating your fact in a way that seems clearly to be doing so for a different purpose than that of playing the game. Let us assume that the give-away clue is that your murderer has dyed his moustache. You could provide an easy clue by having your detective remark to his Watson, 'There is the matter of the colour of Dr Demulch's moustache.' Or you could hover angel-like behind your detective and write, 'He saw that Dr Demulch's moustache was of a deep, homogenous brown colour.' But it would be less obvious to produce a whole description of Dr Demulch in perhaps a mildly humorous vein: 'Dr Demulch was a brown man. His suit was coffee-coloured. His shoes were of a brilliant and gleaming tan. His hair was made to look even browner by the liberal application of hair-oil. His moustache somehow was yet browner than his hair. Even his enormous spectacles were hornrims of spectacular chest-nutery.' Your readers take in, probably without stopping to think much about it, that they are being treated to a rather over-the-top descriptive passage, and they then 'see without seeing' that dyed moustache.

My example also incorporates another method of conceal-ment, a rather cruder one. You can conceal something by putting it as one item of a considerable list, in the above instance the list of brown things. But your list must seem to be there for a purpose. Let me give you an example, one I remem-ber because years ago when I first read the book I actually pen-etrated the secret. It comes in Dorothy L. Sayers' *The Five Red Herrings*, which is set among a group of artists. So what more natural than, in describing an easel mysteriously deserted by a painter, that the tubes of paint littered on the ground should be mentioned one by one? Most readers begin to skim here. 'Oh yes,' they say, 'a lot of paint tubes there. Dorothy L. must be describing them to put over the dramatic picture of the abandoned easel, but I'll take all that for granted.' So they fail to notice that there is no tube of white paint, whereas in another 'list', Miss Sayers' description of the picture on the easel, mention is made of masses of white clouds. So, infer-ence: the picture had been painted at a time other than it appeared to have been, and had been painted by someone who 'could not have been there'. From this we can learn two other things. First, the fairly simple trick of separating two component parts of a clue by a number of pages. Dorothy Sayers separates her description of the picture and her list of the fallen paints here by only a few pages (which is perhaps why I guessed, for once) but you can see how similar clues can be kept in two parts with dozens of pages between them.

The other thing to be learnt from this example is the business of alibis. Constructing a false alibi is difficult, and the beginner would perhaps be well advised not to make the whole of a book depend on such a device. The problem essentially is that you have got simultaneously to account credibly for someone not being at a certain place at a certain time and to account for them precisely being there. You can see how Dorothy Sayers did it by having the victim being supposed to be actively painting when in fact he was dead, and it is by using some such piece of lateral thinking, making the victim provide the alibi in this instance, that the trick is probably most easily brought off.

Take the advice of a great exponent of the Golden Age of the detective story, John Dickson Carr, creator of Dr Gideon Fell: work backwards. Say to yourself, 'X was at this place at that time, now what can I use that would indicate that he was not?' Then when you come to tell your story in the correct time sequence, with any luck the fact that X was there will not be apparent. Again, the separation device can be brought into play. I used a variant of it in a pastiche of the 1930s story I wrote for the fiftieth anniversary of Collins Crime Club in 1980, *The Murder of the Maharajah*. I stated with authorial authority that only people who knew about the way the murder was committed (a complicated affair using an invented tree-bark that became hard when wetted) could have done it and I implied, but with fearful fair play nowhere explicitly stated, that this knowledge could only have been gained by one of a small circle who had watched the Maharajah play a certain practical joke. Much later in the book I had a small scene in which one character is seen just about to tell the murderer, who was not conceivably present when the Maharajah perpetrated his joke, what had happened. I also took care to make this little scene, in the way that I have described, appear to be part simply of an illustration of the appalling character of the Maharajah. Set out badly like this, it may not seem diabolically clever. But, well wrapped up in the story, the device certainly worked well enough for the crime reviewers of that year to vote the book the Gold Dagger award.

Deception is the name of the game when putting clues in front of a reader. Perhaps the basic technique is relying on what the literary theorists call 'stock responses'. These are the unthinking reactions we all have most of the time to various common facts. Write 'The vicar came into the room' and almost all of us will at once see a vague, beneficent figure blinking owlishly. But, of course, a vicar can in fact be almost any sort of human being. However, you could use that initial unthinking response to the idea 'vicar' to fool your reader, as for instance in a short story, by saying no more about the vicar and elsewhere stating that the murder could have been committed only by a man of enormous physical strength.

A crude example. But the device can be used with considerable subtlety. Take a couple of instances from Agatha Christie, who was marvellously cunning with it. I refrain from naming the books in case you have yet to read them. But consider this: a shot rings out, a man falls to the ground clutching his leg, slowly the red stain seeps out on to his trousers. Stock response: he has been wounded in the leg. But read that brief, deliberately clichéd description again. There is the sound of a shot, yes, but no actual mention of a bullet. There is a man falling, yes, but nowhere is it stated that he fell because his leg had been injured. The red stain appeared: stock response 'blood', but blood in fact has not been mentioned. What has happened is that an alibi has been set up, for a wounded man 'could not' have committed the murder that took place immediately afterwards some distance away.

The other instance: we are told on unimpeachable authority that a woman is looking forward to the birth of her daughter; years later we read of a young man arriving on the scene. So we do not think, 'Ah, this is the mother's child'. Our response to talk of the birth of a daughter is that a daughter was born, provided of course that the talk and the child are separated (that same device) by a long period of time and a reasonable number of pages.

Both these instances are of verbal trickery, using a form of words which most often have one meaning but which, in strict logic, can have another. Employing such devices is a fine test of sheer writing skill, of careful and adroit manipulation of language. It can be a considerable pleasure to the writer engaged in creating the now often somewhat despised simple whodunit.

But there can also be trickery using material clues. Take as an example from a fine writer, not of blueprint detective stories but of detective novels, June Thomson, who prefers this sort of clue to the purely verbal ones. In her *A Question of Identity* she gives us early on a good description of a room in a cottage. 'Right,' you say, 'this is to show me what sort of a man it is who lives here.' So when a shotgun propped in a corner is mentioned it seems 'stock response' to assume it to be an expected item of a countryman's equipment and consequently of no significance. You take it in for what it seems and forget, as likely as not, the precise detail. But, pages later, there arises the question of where the weapon came from. Inspector Finch looks for it in various places. We look with him. And all the time the gun has been put right under our noses, just as Poe's letter was hidden in a letter-rack.

Agatha Christie's many clues involving mirrors are of this material type. By lifting these and other examples out of the compelling context of the stories in which they are embedded and analysing just how they are weaved in you will probably be able to see how, in the compelling story you are contemplating, a similar device can be used.

But note, too, as you examine such clues in the hands of masters of the craft, that almost always they put down their clues with a fine boldness. You can easily enough slip in a clue in two quick words somewhere, but when at the end of a book you say that your detective solved the case from noticing that one briefly-stated fact, the reader will experience a sense of let-down. No, your clue should be boldly planted, but while it is a dandelion you should give the reader the impression it is a daffodil. Read Agatha Christie's *Death on the Nile* and note the way she makes Poirot time and again call attention to a pistol that has been thrown into the river. It is, once you see it 'the right way up', the clue to the whole mystery. But by sheer adroitness of writing Dame Agatha has prevented us seeing it as such.

Finally, here are two other methods of giving and not giving the reader a clue, besides burying it in a list of casual items, separating it into two with a wide gap between the parts or appearing, in putting it in, to be doing something else. First, a trick I learnt from a newspaper article about a discovery in psychology. If, it appears, you tell a subject to watch out for a certain item in a series of random sights the subject will seldom be able to recall whatever immediately preceded the watched for item. You can adopt this device for your own evil purposes. Have your detective say it is very important to tell whether something is or is not done in a certain way; then show that thing being done in either of the ways mentioned; but immediately before that happens put in, quite boldly, what it is you want to slip past your reader. The chances are that it will be 'seen and not seen'.

And, almost the opposite effect, lay your clue before your readers decently clearly, and at once follow it with a burst of action. Have, in the classic phrase of Raymond Chandler, a man come in the door with a gun, make your detective then run for his life or chase the gun-toting man. In the flurry and excitement your clue will bulk much less large in the reader's mind than it would have done.

The Murder

All this has been, so to speak, a mere preliminary to the central act of a murder story, the murder, and there are a number of things we should consider about this murder and the murderer. First, a murder should be, as far as you can make it so, attention-grabbing. We have already seen that a murder is necessary in a detective story, if only to tell the reader that this is something worth attention. So it follows that the more startling or bizarre your murder is, within reason, the better. Remember how Dorothy L. Sayers started her career in *Whose Body?*: with the corpse of a stranger in someone's bath 'with nothing on but a pair of pince-nez'. And 44 years later P. D. James starts her novel of detection, *Unnatural Causes*, 'The corpse without hands lay in the bottom of a small sailing dinghy drifting just within sight of the Suffolk coast.'

But, of course, having hit on your attention-grabbing murder, bizarre but not so bizarre that you risk spluttering giggles instead of riveting attention, you have to account for how your curious event came about. You have, in other words, to invent your plot. One of the earliest jottings I made when I began to keep a crime-writing notebook concerned just this business of plot. 'The Switch-point,' I wrote. 'There needs to be some factor which when seen in its true light makes the reason for the murder obvious, but which is more easily seen in a false light.' In those days, I believe, the expression 'lateral thinking' had not been invented. But it exactly describes what you need to achieve: something that the reader, unless lucky enough to make that sideways jump of the mind, will not be able to see.

It is perhaps slightly easier for the writer than for the

reader. Because the writer can do what John Dickson Carr advocated: think backwards. So you start out from some curious notion you have hit on, or even not so curious. Say that the wrong person has been murdered, a basic idea that has been used and used again but which, given other fresh aspects to your book, can very well be made to serve once more. Then you ask how it might have come about that the murderer made that mistake, and already, when eventually you tell of this from the other end, from the discovery of the corpse, you have got something that will require a reader to make a lateral jump to see what really happened.

But it is perhaps better not to try to make a bizarre idea for a murder the seed in your mind for a book, though when you have devised your plot you should of course make the actual circumstances of the murder as attention-grabbing as possible. All too easily, if you pin the whole plot on something that seems to you a tremendous novelty, you can find that some writer you haven't happened to read has had much the same idea before you. Nicholas Blake, the poet C. Day Lewis, once told me with remembered acute dismay how that had happened to him. Incautiously taking what seemed a marvellous idea from a friend, the notion of two people who wished to get rid of someone swapping victims, he discovered when his book was written that this was precisely the plot of a novel by Patricia Highsmith, *Strangers on a Train*, which neither he nor his friend knew of. So the more you invest in curious methods of murder—your melting ice-dagger, your piano-key trigger—the more you increase the risk that some ingenious author has been there before you.

No, for both the classical detective story and other forms it is better to try and find a plot that arises from something else you want to write about, a particular sort of person you know, a setting you know or want to find out about, even an idea about life. So, when I found I wanted to write a book that would reflect a little on whether we should strive to be perfect or settle for the second-best but practical, I realised I would have to have a murder that was in some way imperfect. This led me to look at various conventional sorts of murder which could be seen as being ideal or perfect murders, with the notion of reversing one of them. At last I hit on something as obvious as the bash with the heavy candlestick and decided that the murderer would use the weapon the wrong way up, that is, in a highly imperfect manner. So he would, in fact, not quite kill his victim, thus committing an imperfect murder. And from this kernel notion I developed the plot of my first Inspector Ghote novel called—wait for it— *The Perfect Murder.*

Another warning about what sort of murder you choose: beware hermeneutic error. I came upon this trumpeting word, as far as I remember, listening to a talk about detective fiction on Radio Three (where else?). In principle, hermeneutics is a branch of theology, the study in the Bible and elsewhere of the hidden significance of outward manifestations. But the speaker on Radio Three applied it, very nicely, to what happens in a detective story that is never described by the writer. And this is, most often, the actual murder.

You devise a fine, curious way for your murderer to do his deed, but all that you actually describe to the reader is the resultant body, struck all over with porcupine quills or whatever. Fine. You can make that description properly attention-grabbing. But when you get to the end of your book and your detective explains why the poor chap had to be murdered with porcupine quills your readers are likely to start trying to imagine what happened when the murder took place. And, in all probability, their imaginations will, as they say, boggle because, as you have never seen that scene in your mind's eye, it may well be riddled with improbabilities if it is not a downright impossibility.

So it's not a bad idea to write this scene, even knowing you cannot incorporate it in your final manuscript. In writing, you will discover what can and cannot be done, and then perhaps you will have to modify your attention-grabbing murder, if only by having a few fewer porcupine quills.

The lesson of the porcupine quills (and for an actual example of how not to do it read my *Zen There Was Murder*, if after all these years you can find a copy) is that any part of your book that you do not directly present to the reader ought to be thought out in imaginative terms, just as thoroughly as you have used your imagination to make whatever you have written fully credible.

Here is a rather stern injunction I addressed to myself in my notebook on this subject. It is perhaps a good way of avoiding the hermeneutic error. 'Write out what the situation is as seen by each major character. A writer really envisaging the whole of his situation would, I suppose, not need to do this. If it was *all* real to him it could not contain any factual inconsistencies.' It is no bad thing, in fact, to write a sort of essay about each of your main characters, saying as much about their whole lives as you can. Much of what you invent will not appear in the final book (it shouldn't, unless it's relevant to the actual story) but doing this will help you to be absolutely consistent throughout. I wish I could say that I invariably carry out my own advice.

A couple more points need to be considered about the murder. First, when should it happen? It is simplest to have it right at the beginning, like P. D. James' first words, 'The corpse without hands lay in the bottom of a small sailing dinghy.' This is the way you will be thinking, using this sequence: a murder is committed, the detective arrives, the question is at once asked, 'Who might have done it?'. The simple logical progression. It helps you, the writer. It helps the reader.

But perhaps for the particular plot you have arrived at, the particular murder you have in mind, a good deal will have to be told to the reader about pre-murder events. You may well, for instance, be depending to a large extent on the character of the victim (as I was in *The Murder of the Maharajah*) and the least troublesome way to put that character before the reader is in direct scenes showing the future victim in action.

You may need several such scenes. Well and good. But without the murder having happened you have lost that most powerful weapon in your armoury, the simple 'Who-dun-it?' Your readers are not at once asking that onwards-dragging question which should be at the back of their minds all the time. Perhaps if you are one of nature's good novelists whatever you write will hold the reader's attention fixed. (The first dozen pages of one of Simenon's novels *Maigret's Pickpocket*, just describe, for instance, Maigret riding a bus to work and one is simply gripped.) But lesser mortals are apt to need a few crutches.

Here are some:

● in one way or another tell your reader that murder is to be committed 'at the Old Grange before the month is out' and then you will have introduced the who-will-be-done question;

● have an unsuccessful murder attempt (and if you're Agatha Christie, make its victim prove to be the murderer);

● have some lesser crime precede the murder;

● have threats made, either veiled or clear. (This may seem old hat, but I used it, successfully I think, in *Inspector Ghote Draws A Line* in 1979.);

● use humour, so that even if what you write cannot totally grip it at least amuses;

● describe an interesting background, interestingly;

● put your about-to-be suspects and victim through a series of quarrels. (Ding-dong dialogue is among the easier things to write.)

Finally, however much you delay the moment of murder, let it happen by at least one-third of the way through your story. First-class writers can defy this rule-of-thumb, but anyone else doing so risks alienating readers who have come to them for a particular sort of entertainment.

I have said: the moment of murder. But you do not have to confine yourself to just one murder. I like to do so myself when I write this sort of book, out of a feeling that a certain elegant economy goes well with the genre. But Agatha Christie frequently used two murders, and in her *An Autobiography* (another book you ought to read, if only to see what direct, simple writing can do) she recommends a second killing as giving a useful fillip when there is a danger of a story flagging. A tip, incidentally, that reminds us that the whodunit is by no means only a puzzle for the reader to solve before the author lets out the answer, but also and always a story. Dame Agatha, however much people hymned her baffling ingenuity, never forgot this.

Locked rooms

The blueprint detective story to be successful with its readers, even if they do not realise what is being done with them, must have as much of 'story' in it as of 'detective'; even in that most puzzle-oriented sub-genre, the locked-room mystery.

This sort of plot is, in a way, the ultimate temptation to any writer who has ever toyed with producing detective fiction. It seems to be the very purest form of the art, even though it cannot be other than a minor branch of it. Partly this may be due to that hidden psychological impact we have touched on before. Locked chambers go back to that pair of ancient riddles, 'What is the room you leave before entering? What is the room you enter without leaving?' Answers: the womb and the tomb. Step forward, Sigmund Freud. And partly, on a more mundane level, the puzzle of how a murder could have been committed in what John Dickson Carr used to call a 'hermetically sealed chamber' is perhaps the most intriguing one in the detection writer's whole bag of tricks.

Beginners would be well advised to keep off, but if you cannot prevent yourself indulging (and, of course, there is as much pleasure in the devising as in the unravelling) read Chapter 17 of Dickson Carr's *The Hollow Man*. An absolutely blatant digression, it is nothing less than a lecture on the whole idea of locked rooms. And take another tip from me: have your locked-room mystery as a side-issue to your main story as I did in *The Perfect Murder*, my first Ghote book. Then if your idea turns out to be not as magnificently ingenious as when, in the dark hours you first thought of it, all is not lost.

Again, the secret is to think backwards. Devise your method and then tell your story, which inevitably will make the mystery seem rather better than it has to be, because all locked rooms are variants of a small number of simple devices, most of which are ways of making such rooms unlocked all along. But there is scope yet for hundreds more such stories, ingenious variants of the basic few, achieved frequently by the process we have talked about, telling the reader something while apparently telling something else.

Here are some of the main basic devices:

- have your 'murder' prove only an accident, if an extraordinarily unlikely one (This essentially is the secret of Poe's *Murders in the Rue Morgue*);

- lock and even bolt the door of your room from the outside by means of ingenious wires etc.;

- make your murder a suicide who to spite the world contrives that the weapon 'disappears' (I did this in *Go West, Inspector Ghote*, basing the details on a real, and alas quite quickly solved, case which I was told about by a forensic scientist in California);

- play with the time at which the room was locked, by using some clever variant, for instance, on that hoary device the altered clock;

- have the victim hexed, by whatever is the most up-to-date method, into committing suicide having first locked himself or herself in;

- have the hermeticalness of your room 'vouched for' by a character not of accepted reliability, though seeming to be so.

Looked at in a cold light, most of these devices seem pretty silly, if not worse. But given the necessary criteria, that the puzzle should be impossible but after all possible, it is hard to see how anything better could be contrived. The art lies, in fact, not so much in the contriving as in the telling afterwards. I will add simply that locked rooms are only the purest of all sorts of 'impossible crimes'. (Example: Julian Symons' widely anthologised short story *As If By Magic*, about a murder on the pier in which the killer is bound to have horribly bloodied his jacket but where no one can be seen in such a state. Solution: a Punch-and-Judy booth is a fine and private changing-room.)

By and large everything I have said about locked rooms applies to 'impossible crimes' and they can be as fascinating to invent as to read. The basic necessity, as with the more conventional murder mystery, is to propound your impossibility with a bang at the very beginning. Then you have that tug which will keep a reader with you wherever you need to go.

Story and form

I cannot end this consideration of the basic puzzle mystery, the blueprint, without drawing attention to two fundamentals which may not at first seem necessary ingredients: story and form. Story I have mentioned more than once already. But there is one more thing at least that needs to be said about it.

It is this. That the blueprint detective story at its most basic is not a story. It is a static puzzle. Someone has been murdered in mysterious circumstances: how has it come about? But this basic situation, in order to be made into something which people will have pleasure in reading, has to be seen in almost the exactly opposite light, as the gradual making clear of things. In other words, as a story. So what has to happen, ideally, is that your detective must learn piece by piece things which will eventually make the answer to the fundamental puzzle clear. But this cannot be a simple step-by-step process. The whole point of this sort of book is that the solution when it comes should be startling and unexpected.

Let me quote a stern rebuke one of my own books once received from an American academic, one Thomas Ozro MacAdoo: 'It is an axiom of detective fiction that each stage of the detective's investigation must produce enough information to allow the reader to indulge in some tentative speculation as to the ultimate outcome.' Slap!

So you have a pretty difficult problem, or series of problems, in front of you. Which is why just now I used the word 'ideally'. In practice, you probably have to err this way and that as you tell your story, sometimes risking the reader learning too much, sometimes risking losing interest by not giving the reader the feeling that there is enough material for tentative speculation.

One of the most obvious ways of telling a story which has to arise from the fact of a mysterious murder is to have your reader watch your detective conducting interviews with each of the suspects in turn. This does fulfil the essential of making your hero gain some useful fact from each scene you show him or her in, though the danger for the tyro plotter is that at the end of each interview one more suspect will have simply been 'written out'. No, what the detective *should* gain from such interviews is something pointing suspicion at someone other than the suspect being interviewed.

Beware, however, of a succession of interviews and nothing else which, while corresponding perhaps to a real-life investigation, can become rather repetitive in pattern and thus boring, even in the hands of such a skilled practitioner as Ngaio Marsh who often laid out her books on these lines. So, from time to time, 'have a man come in the door with a gun', as Raymond Chandler famously said, or have another murder committed, as Dame Agatha famously did.

As a way of tackling the major problem of making something essentially static into something always forward-moving, I offer this tip. In the early stages of a book I always write out two things: one, the plot, that is, the murder and how it happened and perhaps how eventually it will be seen for what it is; two, the story (which to make what I mean even clearer to myself I generally label 'The Storyline'), that is, in very rough outline what happens first and what happens next and next and next. Story basically is just the 'and nexts' one after another.

So, finally, form. Form is one of the hidden assets of the detective story. It is not something which your average reader is even particularly aware of (unless he happens to be French). But, as in life when you enter a room that has balance and shape in its architecture, it is something that has a subtle and decidedly enhancing effect.

In contrast to the mainstream novel, which tends to be all sprawl, it is essential for the blueprint detective story to have shape. It begins with a single central fact, the murder; it broadens out as suspect after suspect comes into play; then almost at the last moment it narrows abruptly down to another single fact, the murderer. Of course, you can achieve variations on this basic form, if only by having a second murder and getting a shape rather like a violin. But the thing to remember is that this quality of form exists and that, whether readers acknowledge it or not, a marked shape or form, as in the 'nursery rhyme' books of Agatha Christie, considerably adds to their pleasure.

So while your book is in the early malleable stage, remember form and see if you cannot arrange things to good advantage. And then. . . . Then tell the story. Tell the story. I often think this is the most useful single piece of advice to give any would-be novelist. It got firmly and finally stamped into my head on one never-to-be-forgotten occasion. An American publisher friend had asked if she could bring her travelling companion when I had asked her to dinner. The companion turned out to be that marvellous novelist, Eudora Welty, and in the course of the evening she talked about how, when she was a child in the American South, people would come back from market, or whatever, and delight in telling those present what they had happened to see. Eudora Welty said this was how she had learnt the secret of fiction writing.

So, as you write, think of who you are talking to, and *tell* them what you want them to hear.

2
The Modern Variations

Deeply though a great deal of crime fiction today is rooted in the blueprint detective story, there is now only a small public for such books in their pure form and, I think, there are not so many writers who want to produce them. Whether it is that nowadays people are less interested in playing games as between author and reader, or whether it is that the human liking for games-playing has been transferred to other fields I do not know. But the fact is that gradually from the heyday of the detective story in the 1920s, '30s and '40s new tendencies crept in.

It may have been that writers felt that every variation in their particular game had been played, but recognised that a public appetite for detection had been created and would repay feeding. Or it may have been that, looking at the blueprint form, some of them saw that something more could be done with it. It is a process in literature that has occurred in the past in other fields. You could say that out of the simple song there came the poem capable of expressing in a short length deep thoughts. Or you could say that from the story told under the palm-tree or round the winter hearth there developed the novel.

So for various reasons slightly different sorts of detective fiction came to be written and after a while came to be acknowledged as viable in their own right. More, they came to be models which readers wanted and, for most of them, which readers still want.

There was what has come to be called the inverted story, that is, a mystery which begins with the murderer being seen to commit the murder and in which the interest lies in seeing how he will not get away with it despite that apparent perfection of his method. Then there was what we might call the back-grounder, the detective story in which interest lies as much in the setting as in the puzzle. There was, too, the how-dun-it, the book in which it soon becomes evident who the murderer is but in which he or she cannot be brought to satisfying justice unless some ingenious, proof-defying method used is brought to light.

There was as well, similar but a whole step in advance the why-dun-it, the book which depends for its interest on showing that someone who could easily enough have committed a certain murder but who on the face of it was incapable of that particular crime (i.e. one who had J. C. Masterman's aces of spades, hearts and diamonds but apparently not clubs) is nevertheless seen eventually to be psychologically capable of that crime after all, once probed deeply enough.

There was, again, with the passing of time, the sort of book it is convenient to call the detective novel as opposed to the detective story, though publishers' blurb writers have so abused the terms that they have become almost indistinguishable. But by the detective novel I mean a book in which the puzzle element is reduced and in which the characters are a good deal more lifelike than those which the blueprint puzzle merchants needed and in which the element of character drawing is given much more weight. Finally, there came the crime novel, a development of the detective novel with the emphasis yet more on the characters and often and especially on their milieu. Still retaining the essential element of a crime and still being primarily entertainment, this frequently will have no puzzle element as such.

Let us now look at each of these kinds of books in turn and see what we can about how they are written. Note first, however, that categories being the invention of critics and books being the creation of writers, seldom will any of these sub-genres of crime fiction be without something of the others in it.

The inverted story

The earliest examples of this type in which the identity of the murderer is no longer a secret to be kept till the closing pages pre-date the blueprint detective story's heyday. They are a collection of short stories, *The Singing Bone*, published in 1912 and written by R. Austin Freeman, a formidable advocate of the detective story as an exercise in rigorous logic, who once wrote that the ideal reader should be 'a clergyman of studious and scholarly habit' and that the most interesting pages must be those of the final explanation. In this small group of tales he first described in the third person how a murder had happened and then in the voice of his 'Watson' narrated the activities of his sleuth Dr Thorndyke, the scientist, in bringing the murderer to book. There is a certain peculiar fascination in the stories. The mere recounting of difficult feats, here of forensic science though any arduous achievement will do, well told in unfolding detail will grip a reader nine times out of ten. But the stories never swept the reading public off its feet the way the Sherlock Holmes tales did.

So it was many years later, in 1930, that a writer of light-hearted detective stories called Anthony Berkeley proclaimed that the art should change from puzzles about time, place and opportunity into puzzles about motive and character, and produced a book, *The Second Shot*, written from the murderer's point of view. This he quickly followed up with two books, written under the name Francis Iles, *Malice Aforethought* and *Before the Fact*, both with clear acknowledgement from the start of the identity of the murderer. They have become classics in our field, and, once again, you should read them if you have not already done so.

Paradoxically, much of what I have said about the writing of straightforward mystery stories applies just as much to inverted stories, the books that seemingly set out on an exactly opposite course. The whodunit tug is, of course, replaced by the where-did-he-go-wrong tug. And it is important to keep as firmly in mind that this is what the reader wants to know, as it was in writing the blueprint detective story to remind oneself constantly that what the reader is looking for is hints towards answering the question 'Who did it?'.

Yet more paradoxically, in a book where the mystery has, so to speak, been given away from the start there still has to be 'fair play'. There is still an unwritten contract the writer has with the reader. Only here what must be put squarely, if not exactly clearly, before the reader is what it is that will after all betray the murderer. Again, the motive you assign to your murderer must be credible, and the various suggestions I have already made about motive could well help if you decide to plan a story on the inverted system.

You will too, of course, need a detective, and the same limitations and assets that the detective in the classical story has will still apply to the detective here. Curiously enough, provided the mystery to be solved is not feeble and provided you can manage to write about its solution vividly, the fact that your reader already knows the murderer's identity will matter very little. You can prove this for yourself, in fact, by re-reading any good whodunit where you can remember who the murderer eventually proved to be. Try it with the best Agatha Christies. It is quite as fascinating seeing 'how she done it' as eventually discovering who said she done it.

Again, in putting fairly before your reader all that your detective sees in the hunting down of your known murderer, everything that we have said about concealing yet revealing clues still applies. Equally, your murder still needs to be, in so far as you can contrive it without becoming ridiculous, attention-grabbing. But here, luckily, you will be spared the difficulty that can arise through not having 'seen' that murder since in all probability you will have begun your story by describing, in as much vivid and convincing detail as you can manage, the killing itself or its immediate circumstances as they affect the perpetrator.

One problem we have discussed as affecting the writer of the blueprint detective story is likely to be even more acute when embarking on an inverted story: the difficulty of making a static situation into an ongoing narrative. Because here your situation, the murder that has been committed, is if anything more static, and your detective's progress towards unravelling it is liable to become a rather dull series of minor discoveries, often arising from interviews which tend to be similar in pattern. But, again, such devices as the second murder can be used to give the reader a necessary shock. The second murder, too, will have to occur because your murderer, rightly (or even better, wrongly) suspects the detective is getting too close for comfort or that one of the other characters has hit on something they ought not, from his point of view, to have done. This you will describe, of course, as seen through the murderer's eyes.

The backgrounder

This is a type of book that crept almost unremarked into the field. Quite early in the history of detective fiction its writers began to feel that the mere producing of one yet more ingenious murder was not enough, that perhaps setting a slightly less ingenious murder in some interesting area would give readers an extra reason for staying with the book. The chief exponent of this sort of story was, of course, Dorothy L. Sayers.

She may have been led to the variations by the necessarily high-class backgrounds of her Lord Peter's earlier investigations, but the book in which she definitively arrived at the backgrounder was *The Five Red Herrings* of 1931, in which murder takes place in an artists' colony in Galloway in Scotland. Following this came the two great classic examples, *Murder Must Advertise*, set in an advertising agency, and *The Nine Tailors*, with its background of church bellringing.

Both these, of course, also have underneath the pattern of the blueprint detective story and all that we have seen about that sort of book applies to the backgrounder, though perhaps with less rigour. But what of this new element of background? The first thing to be said about it is that, whatever background you choose, it must mesh in well with the murder plot. It is not enough to think of a murder and who committed it and why that is not immediately obvious, and then to take some setting that seems interesting and simply introduce chunks of description from time to time. If you do, your readers are likely to feel cheated.

No, the way to get at it is to work from whatever background has fired your imagination. And fired is the word. If you look around for some field that has yet to be used in a crime story and then insist on using it when it has not filled you with enthusiasm, your book will be leaden. But, given a subject, a place, a community, a way of life, that you find actively interesting, then you should begin by brooding over its possibilities. Ask yourself what in its particular essence could possibly cause a murder to happen, or what sort of murder might arise out of this particular place or community or life-style. Then off you go. Your background will of necessity permeate the story you eventually tell.

Let me give an instance from my own writing life. The first few crime books I wrote failed to sell to any American publisher. Time and again the report came back 'Too British.' So I began to think how I could write a crime story that did not have a British setting. India in those days (round about 1963) was much in the air and I found that as a background it decidedly fired my imagination. So, I thought, how about a murder puzzle set in India? But what particular sort of murder did India seem to prescribe to me? More thought. Then I saw it: India as a place where things frequently were less than perfect. Being less than perfect matched with being as perfect as possible was one of the human conundrums that also fired my imagination. So, as I have recounted already, there came into being *The Perfect Murder*, which turned out to be the first of my books to be published in America.

I had not at that time ever been to India. To write about a place I did not know might seem to be breaking one of the most quoted warnings to the novice author: 'Write about what you know'. It's a good rule, but I think it needs to be looked at a little more closely. Of course you can make appalling howlers if you set out for some reason to portray life in a social area unknown to you. I can recall to this day a book I had for review years and years ago in which the hero swaggered into a smart London night club, ordered a magnum of champagne and drank it down. Well, a magnum sounds splendidly sophisticated, but it does hold as much as two ordinary bottles. So I doubt if our hero would have been good for many heroics after swigging that.

However, if some setting that you have little or no first-hand experience of does happen to be what has made your imagination bubble and race, you need not cross it off altogether. After all, there are few areas of human experience that have not been written about, and you can experience your chosen one through other writers' words just as well, perhaps even in some ways actually better, than through your own eyes. Nor need your eyes miss seeing what your feet perhaps cannot take you to. Television exists, and it's surprising how, if you search the columns of the journals, sooner or later you come across programmes about almost anything.

They may not be directly concerned with whatever you want to know about, but they will often put it before your very eyes. I once garnered a useful titbit about Indian life from a documentary about the highest balloon flight in the world because I happened to see that it took place in the centre of the Indian sub-continent where the air can be particularly still. But let me warn you: it is not easy to watch a programme on television or a film in the cinema or on video for a reason other than the one it is being put out for. To discount the commentary or, worse, the story and look like a hawk at the passing background requires no little effort of concentration.

But, if you do find yourself in the situation of describing an area of life you are unfamiliar with, remember the man with the magnum of champagne and avoid, as far as you possibly can, using any fact, however trivial, however seductive, that you have no warrant for in someone else's words or pictures.

The how-dun-it

The detective story with an interesting background is not so far removed from the classical original. Nor is this particular variation, the story in which the interest lies in *how* a baffling murder of some sort can have been committed. Essentially, everything is much the same as in the classical template except that in all probability it will be pretty well apparent to the reader quite soon who it is who has committed the murder. You will not need to take as many steps to conceal this as you would have had you been writing the blueprint book. What you will have to protect, with all the ingenious means we have looked at, is just how this murder you have devised was committed. You replace, in other words, the who-did-it tug with the how-on-earth-was-it-done tug.

It is, I think, a somewhat less magnetic question. But if your mind runs to ingenuities of physical fact, then it is a type of book that can still attract readers. As before, the essential trick is working backwards and writing forwards.

Suppose some little physical fact has struck you; for instance, a green dress seen under a red light can look black. So you devise a situation where an absolutely unimpeachable witness sees the murderer in black leaving the scene of the crime. Then you tell the story of the murder and the subsequent investigation, adroitly working in the fact that there was a red light shining at the vital time and place, using one of the ways of tricking your reader into 'noticing and not noticing' this that we looked at in the previous chapter, and you also harp like mad on the impossibility of a person in a black dress or suit having been on hand at the moment the murder was committed. (You had better find a cleverer central device for a book than my example, though.)

The why-dun-it

We move now to a larger departure from the blueprint; books in which the tug factor is not who did it but *why* such-and-such a person committed some particular crime; books in which the emphasis is on character.

Writers of the so-called Golden Age of the detective story, the 1920s, '30s and '40s, are often denigrated for using cardboard characters. Most writers of the blueprint books of that time certainly did present the would-be solvers of their puzzles with little more than cut-out figures labelled 'Millionaire', 'Unfaith-ful Wife', 'Devoted Secretary', although of course the better writers of the time were far from such crudities. But there is not, in fact, one huge divide set between cardboard characters on the one hand and characters in depth on the other.

All novelists go deeper and less deep into their various char-acters as the needs of their novel dictate. A writer such as Agatha Christie, often the target of ill-informed criticism over this, is well capable, where she can afford to do so, of drawing people of some complexity with contradictions in their behav-iour and hidden layers under the surface. In writing the why-dun-it you will need to draw characters of varying depth so that your readers can share with you the delights of analysis.

But with the introduction of this new and quite different element we, as it were, at last cast aside the painter that tied our boat to the safe bank of blueprint detective fiction. We are afloat now, and much more at the mercy of the capricious tides of the writer's imagination.

Or at least we would be if were were about to produce the full-out why-dun-it. However, a great many books that, if one were tabulating them by content, would perhaps have to be called why-dun-its still have in them considerable ele-ments of other sub-genres. You are by no means obliged to cast in your lot one hundred percent with any critics-made category, though it is well worth while when your book is still an idea vaguely moving in your head to decide what sort of a book it is on the whole. Otherwise you may find yourself later, as you sweep along on the actual business of writer, gradually drifting into producing quite another sort of book than the one you set out to write and in consequence disap-pointing readers' expectations which at the beginning you had gone to trouble to arouse. Believe me, this can happen. I have read for review, but not usually in the end reviewed, not a few books where this seems to have occurred.

However, let us assume that you have decided on a full-out why-dun-it. You have been gripped by the urge to write a book in which there will be a murder with a murderer not immediately apparent but whose identity will eventually be made clear because of some idiosyncracy in his or her mental make-up.

Some of the canons of the classical form still apply. You still have an essentially static situation (X killed Y because X was such-and-such a person) and you still therefore have the

problem of presenting that situation to your readers in a progressive way.

But now what you will have bit by bit to show them is not
a series of physical clues or eliminating alibis but, chiefly, the
character of your murderer. Instead of writing a story in
which, say, at some crucial point the detective realises that the
gun beside the corpse is not the one that fired the fatal shot,
you will be writing a story in which the detective will perhaps
realise that the theory of the murder being motivated by
greed cannot be correct because the suspect has been found
unexpectedly to be secretly most generous.

So you must contrive a number of situations in which character is revealed, either directly in talk or in action or in what
other people in your book, the vestigial 'other suspects', have
to say. Because of the nature of this sort of book you can afford
to let the identity of the murderer become more obvious much
earlier than if you were writing the classical blueprint.

Of course, you will have to have a detective through whom
the reader will watch this gradual revelation. This is the sort
of book in which the amateur detective, modern-style, is a
much more credible figure. It is by no means altogether
improbable, for instance, that some ordinary person on the
periphery of a murder should be so disturbed by some apparent contradiction of character that he or she feels obliged to
talk about it to others involved, and thus gradually comes to
unearth the secret of character you have put at the heart of
your story. Read a few of the later books of that excellent
author Elizabeth Ferrars to see how plausible this can be
made to be.

And, once again, you will see that you have had to work
backwards. You have been struck by some particular type of
person and have found a plausible set of circumstances in
which a person of that type would commit a murder. But now
you have to begin at the other end and tell the story in a
straight run through the eyes, or over the shoulder, of the
'detective' figure.

If you possibly can, tell the story through these eyes or
other eyes. It will act as a barrier to you in putting your own
psychological discoveries directly to your reader. Unless you
are a raving genius, doing that is not a good idea. A reader
will be prepared to accept an insight if it is presented as fiction, that is, as something a fictional character observes. But
that same reader is likely to resent and disbelieve the same

insight when it is told him as a fact by an author. The insight, indeed, gets tested for truth by the very business, paradoxically, of writing it out as fiction.

The detective novel

With our boat's painter trailing in the shadows behind us, let us now move on to look at what I have called the detective novel as opposed to the detective story. The distinction, though in practice it is often blurred, in theory is clear. The detective story is a book written with the sole purpose of showing the reader an act of detection and inviting that reader to a battle of wits in arriving at the solution before the author makes it known. The detective novel is partly a novel, an exploration of some facet of human existence, and partly an account of an act of detection used to keep the reader reading, to provide the essential storyline. A parallel example, if you like, is the way in which Jane Austen used the courtship story in order to write novels, considerations of aspects of the human predicament such as pride and prejudice or sense and sensibility.

Along with the crime novel, which we shall consider shortly, the detective novel is perhaps the most commonly written form of crime fiction today. It is the one most writers seem to want to embark upon, the one most readers seem to want to read. But, again, it will not be as easy to lay down rules for writing it, since it is basically a version of the blueprint detective story but with all its rules loosened.

One thing, however, it is possible to say squarely. The difference between a simple detective story and a novel is that the novel has—sometimes unknown to the author—a theme. It is about something. (Some less good novels are about more than one thing, and are the less good for that.) So this is an altogether new factor when we come to the detective novel. The detective novel must be about something. And, unless you are that raving genius we have met before, you would do well to analyse exactly what it is your detective novel is about before you embark on detailed plotting, let alone the actual writing.

Let us say that it occurs to you that a story in which a husband kills his wife without any apparent motive would be 'a marvellous idea'. The unmotive you have vaguely hit on turns out to be that the fellow was obsessively jealous of his wife who was, as would be evident to everybody else, so obsessively faithful to him that no question of jealousy could arise. The whole idea seems bubblingly exciting to you. Now stop. Ask yourself what such a story is about, what is the kernel of it. The answer will be: jealousy. The notion of jealousy fires your imagination; you feel you have something to say on the theme. Well and good. You have got the fire in your belly that will make an excellent detective novel. Provided that, as you develop the original idea, you keep it in mind constantly that jealousy is your theme. You need other people who could have killed the wife, your essential suspects. Try to build them out of other aspects of jealousy.

Another tip from my crimewriting notebook, one garnered from an academic study of the novel, *The Heyday of Sir Walter Scott* by Professor Donald Davie. The story you choose should reflect the theme you want to write about. When things are still fluid in your mind, ask yourself, 'What exactly is my theme?' And then, 'What is the central action of my story?' In our case this will almost certainly be the murder, since this is a novel based on the detection of a murder. Now ask: 'Is this central action the pivot for my theme?' You may find at this point that you have to adjust your thoughts, if only by a little, to get this ideal equation properly lined up. You might, for instance, have to alter the way the murder you had in mind is committed or you might have to go so far as to alter the motive of the murderer or even find a completely different person to commit the central action.

For the rest, a great deal of what you have to do in the detective novel will be much what the writer of the blueprint story had to do, though in each department there will be modifications. Of course, you will have to have what P. D. James called the mysterious death at the heart of your story. But it will have to be more than the mysterious death used in the old, simple detective story. It should, if your detective novel is going to be truly successful in literary terms, be the simple action on which the theme of the book, whatever that may be, pivots.

Further, it should be now, not so much a bizarre, attention-grabbing death as the murder of someone who is more than a mere blood-bathed cadaver. Your victim should be someone of interest as a person. The deeper the interest the better the book is likely to be. And, of course, this victim should exemplify somehow your theme.

Again, you will have a closed circle of suspects. But now they will be much more human beings like the people we meet in our lives than those stock response, cut-out figures like the Vamp and the Villain (to go for examples to the world of Hindi films). Now you will be able to take advantage, for instance, of making a really sympathetic figure seem so likely to have committed the murder that your readers will be crying out, 'Oh, no, no, don't let it be like that'. But, note, that although your book will be much more like 'real life' than the basic, blueprint formula, you still cannot upset your readers by, as in real life, having the murderer be that passing sex pervert or opportunist small-time thief. You are writing a *detective* novel: you have pledged to your readers that there will be a good measure of detection still.

You will find, unless there are very good reasons for doing otherwise, that here you will find it difficult to manage if you have as many as eight suspects, for no longer can your suspects be mere plaster figures. They must each have something of reality about them. So take a tip from none other than Graham Greene: 'A story hasn't room for more than a limited number of created characters.' I suggest that four suspects as well as your murderer will be quite enough to cope with.

Of course, you will have to have the detective. But now he, or she, needs to be an even broader, more sympathetic figure than before. You will need a detective, be it a police officer or some individual caught up for good reason in the investigation, who is capable of seeing deeply into people's characters, of putting himself like Simenon's Maigret into, not so much other people's shoes, as into other people's minds and souls.

So a word of warning: be careful of relying on a person too far away from yourself. If you embark on using someone as your detective who is immensely superior to yourself either intellectually or in the social scale (and by that I do not mean any conventional listing of dukes, earls, barons and honourables) you will be heading for trouble when you try to have the sort of insights for them that they would naturally have. And, conversely, don't, however attractive the reason, have someone lower in that social pecking-order or less intelligent than yourself.

Agatha Christie recounts in *An Autobiography* how, when she was on the point of creating Poirot, she toyed for just a little with the notion of a schoolboy detective. You can see the attraction, the novelty and the piquancy. But wisely

Mrs Christie saw that she would have much more difficulty seeing the world through juvenile spectacles than she would through Belgian ones. Yet note that the Belgian ones proved, on the whole, perfectly wearable. Your detective does not need to be you yourself just as you are. But he, or she, does need to be within striking distance of yourself, especially when you have set out on the tricky waters of the novel.

With the 'novel' element displacing to a greater or lesser extent the 'detective' element, you will probably find that you need a less complicated murder to be the subject of the logical deduction which will eventually reveal it for what it is. Instead of a plot of intertwined complication, which would do nicely for a book in which its unravelling was the whole of the matter, you might well find that a plot which consisted of only one major twist or deception would suit you best.

Your book now is going to bear much more relation to reality than one in which the murderer has to perform two or three pretty unlikely actions so as to provide the impenetrable mystery. But mystery you still must have. So, one fact seeming to be what it is not, provided it is a fact of decent substance, is likely to meet your case.

I give, a little hesitantly, one example from my own books. *Inspector Ghote Draws a Line* is a story (on the theme of should lines be drawn; should the thin ends of all wedges be repulsed?) in which Ghote is sent to a house in the deep Indian countryside to find out who is threatening with death the old Judge who lives there. Stripped of all the trimmings, the plot depends finally on one 'trick', causing the reader to assume that an ignorant servant could not possibly be the writer of the elaborate legal phraseology of the threatening notes, whereas in fact the fellow has copied the phrases from the legal paraphernalia all about the house. I think this single gimmick was enough to provide the detection element while Ghote's investigations among the more likely looking suspects enabled me, with diversions, to tell my story and to reflect in various ways on lines drawn and wedges advanced.

To tell my story: because I was very conscious that out of the static situation of the servant being the one who was menacing the Judge I had to make an ongoing story. As you will have to. But here the writer of the detective novel has an advantage over the concocter of the detective story. In life, things happen. So in writing about life it is not difficult to have things happen. Your suspects are likely to be opposed to one another in different ways (if they are not, you have chosen people who do not adequately reflect different aspects of your theme) and if they are opposed it is not unlikely that they will quarrel, again about your theme.

Into the less cerebral atmosphere of a detective novel it is unlikely, too, that you will find opportunities for scenes of action, and that they will seem less like seized-on injections of pep-up dope than they would amid the logical probings of the puzzle story. So perhaps this is the place to consider how such scenes should be written.

Action is happenings. And the key therefore to writing scenes of action is to limit yourself as strictly as you can to describing happenings. Do this in detail. Provided that your detail is correct, believable and expressed without hectic, worried adjectives, it is surprising how much simple plain statement will grip a reader. You can see this in the adventure novels of Alastair Maclean; you can see it equally in the intellectual novels of Iris Murdoch. Dame Iris has a fancy for the occasional scene of action, though they always have a meaning, a symbolic resonance for their particular book, and she has, too, a gift for writing them. She does it, when you analyse, in just the way Maclean does. By the solid building up of crisp and exact detail.

Here again I can quote Graham Greene, though he was writing in this instance about the thriller, which is outside the scope of this book. But excitement, he said in one of his autobiographical books, is simple. It should be just described without any wrapping up in metaphor and similes. These, he points out, are reflections, reflections in the mind of the person to whom they occur. But action is when there is no time to reflect. All it wants is a subject, a verb, an object and possibly some rhythm in the prose. And I add: don't fall into the trap of insisting in your own narration that something is exciting, just let the subject-verb-object description do the work for you.

Your detective in the detective novel will, too, have more reason to probe deeply into character during questioning sessions. A real detective superintendent investigating a murder will confine himself largely to facts and only at the height of questioning someone he is almost certain is his quarry is he likely to go into motivation as a way, as often as not, of bringing about a final confession.

But the detective in a detective novel is not altogether your real policeman, though you do well never to make him (if he is a police officer) flout details of proper police procedure. The best way of doing this is perhaps to follow the advice of Ruth Rendell (Read her books) who once said, 'I try not to make errors in my descriptions of police work: I accomplish that largely by leaving it out.' No, your detective will be as much created by the 'novel' element as by the 'detective'. So he will have certain latitudes, because that is what the reader needs. Look for an example of this at P. D. James' Commander Dalgleish. Outwardly he could be in almost every way a Scotland Yard senior officer. Inwardly he is a whole lot more.

One last observation about the detective novel. Ideally your final revelation should combine both the elements of this double-harnessed form, detection and novel writing. At its best such a book will not only provide a satisfying solution to the murder puzzle which it still must have, but also at the same time the solution of the mystery should reveal finally what it was the novel had to say. Note, however, that this should not be as explicit as is the name of the murderer. Your reader should be left only with the feeling that something about life has been made clear.

I have prefaced this last thought with the word 'ideally' since I know it is not something that is at all easy to achieve. But even for the beginner it is worth having in mind the utmost that the sort of book embarked on can reach to. And, as I have said before, the further away we get from the original blueprint formula, the more scope there is for books that do less in some directions and perhaps more in others than the standard design would seem to indicate as being possible.

The crime novel

Nowhere is this more so than in the sub-division of crime fiction that I have labelled the 'crime novel'. Yet, in so far as it can be pinned down, this is the sort of crime fiction that many writers today want to write, and many, many readers want to read. How does it differ from the detective novel?

Answer one: in many cases the two will hardly be distinguishable. Answer two: a crime novel may still be crime fiction, as opposed to pure fiction, even if it abandons altogether that prime staple of blueprint detective fiction, the murder puzzle. A crime novel need not ask that question

'Who done it?' and yet, because its writer has kept in mind the primary duty of entertaining, it will still be something different from the novel that has a crime in it.

In other words, if you have decided to write a crime novel you are absolved from the duty of giving the world another Dostoievsky's *Crime and Punishment*. That was a novel, a novel in which Dostoievsky's sole aim was to put before his readers his thoughts on the theme. The mere fact that it was convenient to do so through a story of a murder and the murderer's subsequent feelings and actions had nothing essential to contribute.

Your task in writing a crime novel will be different. Yes, you will have something that you want to convey: your theme. But you will also at the same time want to give your readers entertainment arising out of the description of some sort of crime. And that, really, is the limit of the rules you will be working under.

Where once you would have had as a matter of necessity a plot with at its heart some intricate deception, often unlikely, now your plot will arise from the characters you want to write about. No longer will you need to work backwards: you can take some crime situation, such as the possibility that your main character has committed a murder, and from there work forwards. Nor is this main character of yours likely to be a detective, of any sort. Mostly you will find that you need simply to write about someone to whom something has happened. Your murder, too—and this you will probably, but not certainly, need to retain to hold your readers' interest—will no longer, of course, be an affair of the poisoned ice-dart but some quite straightforward killing, or even half-killing. So good old classical clues will almost certainly have vanished altogether.

But characters will be much more present, be seen in much greater, convoluted depth even than in the detective novel. And your setting will be even more integrated into your book than was the setting in the sort of story I have called a backgrounder. Almost, the setting, the milieu, here will be what the book is about. And it should be such, drawn so strongly, that your readers will remember it as vividly as anything in any other sort of crime fiction.

But because of the very vagueness of form in the crime novel it is all the more important to bear what it is constantly in mind, and all the more difficult to do so. If whatever it is you feel you have to convey becomes too present in your mind, you will easily forget the duty of entertaining. You will end up having written a novel, not a crime novel.

So what, you ask. Well, so nothing, if the novel you have written is a good one and if nothing that you have done in the way of title, type of story, original laying-out of the situation has not broken that contract with the reader which says, 'This will be a crime novel, it will entertain you first of all though it may cause you a little to think'. So what, if you have produced a masterpiece and lost a piece of entertainment? Well, for one thing, few people want masterpieces all the time. Man cannot live on Dostoievsky alone. An occasional easing-off with, say Julian Symons is not only permissible but positively desirable.

But the chances are, too, that if at the beginning you saw yourself as writing a crime novel and no more, then you will have spoilt the novel you eventually turned out to have produced, as well as causing in a good many of your readers a subtle feeling of disappointment.

What then ensures that you keep within the confines of the crime novel? You can help yourself in this by keeping in mind constantly the reader you are writing for. This may be a specific person. Some writers write with someone they know in mind. Or it may be more vaguely a type of person. 'I like to write,' you may say, 'for clergymen of studious and scholarly habit.' Or it may be even vaguer than that; someone rather like oneself but knowing perhaps a little less. Whatever figure you have in your head, ask at every turn of your book, 'What will the Reader (I always give mine a capital letter in my mind) want next?'

The answer, nine times out of ten, will be: the next event in the story. Story, narrative, is what best keeps a crime novel squarely in the entertainment field and one should never forget it. Some authors are lucky enough to think naturally in terms of story. It seems never to occur to them to put down next anything other than what a reader wants next to know. Others of us have to cultivate this talent, and the way to do it is by constantly asking yourself that question, 'What will the Reader want next'? Remember Eudora Welty.

But, once feeling reasonably happy that you are satisfying this need, the novelist in the crime novel can then be allowed his share. You can so aim your plot that the events you will have to describe reflect on whatever current preoccupation of society it is that has fired your imagination: your theme.

Nothing is barred in the crime novel, however much was barred in the old days of the detective story when, for instance, sexual relations often seemed confined to one person expressing just the discreetest interest in another. Nothing is barred, except that your subject (which is, note, not the same thing as your deeper theme) should involve crime of some sort and that your presentation of it should be in a manner that will entertain, which is almost the same thing as saying it should be through a progressing story.

3
Transatlantic Cousins and Others

So far we have looked at, so to speak, the various direct heirs of that original model, the classical detective story. But the great popularity of that sort of book in the 1920s and 1930s had another effect besides producing the series of direct variants that led eventually to the crime novel. The tension, you might say, generated by that success caused crime fiction also to take a huge lateral leap. A leap, in fact, across the whole Atlantic Ocean, and the whole of the continent of America afterwards. The very success of the highly intricate crime story (a success it had also, of course, in America with writers such as Ellery Queen and Rex Stout) produced in California the toughly direct and forceful private-eye story. Such stories, in the words of Raymond Chandler, one of their great exponents, 'gave murder back to the kind of people who commit it for reasons, not just to provide a corpse.'

The great leap, however, took place long ago, round about 1930, and private-eye stories have since produced progeny of their own, much as the detective story produced that chain of books culminating in the crime novel. The private-eye story has even taken, not one huge lateral leap, but a series of hops which have brought it to British shores. A private-eye story is today one of the clear possibilities open to the would-be writer of crime fiction anywhere.

So what exactly is it? Its origins lie in those cheap American magazines of the '20s and '30s called 'pulps' (because they were printed on cheap wood-pulp paper) whose readers demanded tough stories about tough heroes, hard-boiled heroes as they were then called. For these magazines, and notably for one called *Black Mask*, a number of writers who turned out to possess very high skills began to work. Eventually, authors of the calibre of Dashiell Hammett and Chandler moved on to producing full-length books, based often on their early material in the pulps and always with the hero, the person through whose eyes one saw the story, a private-eye, a shamus, a private investigator, a P.I.

The books were, deservedly, enormously successful and stories in the genre have continued to be written down the years and show no sign of drying up. Where once Hammett and Chandler bestrode the world of Californian crime and corruption like collossuses, now private-eyes like Joseph Hansen's Dave Brandstetter (who happens to be homosexual but is otherwise completely in the classic pattern) and Robert B. Parker's Spenser (who happens to work in Boston and be a gourmet cook) work their contemporary beats in almost exactly the old way.

And, as I have said, the genre, however American in origin, has also successfully crossed back over the Atlantic. Not all British private-eye stories match up to their American counterparts, but it can be done. The stories written by Dan Kavanagh about a London private investigator, Duffy, are just one example to prove that the return journey has been successfully accomplished. So are the novels written by Lisa Cody featuring a girl private-eye, Anna Lee, an altogether credible figure. There are, too, not unsuccessful private-eye stories by British authors set in America such as Basil Copper's Mike Faraday books about an authentic-seeming Los Angeles and, earlier, the books of the prolific James Hadley Chase with a whole variety of heroes. The field is wide open.

What should you do, then, if you take it into your head to provide one more example? First, you should get it clear in your mind just what the private-eye who is the central figure is. He, or in the 1990s almost as often she, is, to begin with, the seeing eye of the story, even more so than the Great Detective was in the days of his triumphs. This is because the detective here is more than the observer that the Great Detective in essence was. The private-eye is a person of action. They investigate by going to places, tackling people, often but not always by shooting or slugging them, and often but not obligatorily so by going to bed with them. They will almost always be in the life you describe what they are as a literary concept, a private investigator, a person with all the freedom of action of the amateur detective of old (see how the blueprint formula still has its influence) but who uses it actively.

I have described the private-eye as a literary concept and

this, as applied to a man in a dirty trench-coat moving in and out of sleazy beds and corrupt gambling dens, may seem to be rather excessive. But, however tough a private-eye is in the pages, he is precisely in the pages, a literary concept. They are, in fact, none other than the knight-errant of the fairy tales (as witness Chandler calling his hero originally Malory, after the author of the *Morte d'Arthur*, and Robert Parker calling his Spenser, after the poet of *The Fairy Queen*). They are the lone crusader righting wrongs, rescuing damsels, killing dragons. And, however disreputable the world you move them through, it is as well at the very back of the mind to remember this. It will often enough tell you what it is they should do next.

It is almost obligatory that the private-eye should be a person who looks at society from below, as contrasted with the Great Detective who certainly hovered over the world of murder from high above. James Sandoe, a fine American critic of crime fiction, once said of the typical private-eye that, although there was no specific reason for it, somehow he always had to have a shabby office with 'a shabby restaurant nearby serving leaden eggs and greasy bacon'. Of course, this is not absolutely obligatory. But the shabbiness does indicate one other quality that is obligatory; the private-eye must be a person of integrity. They may not exactly obey every letter of the law. They may sleep around and shoot about. But, because of the sort of story they are embedded in, integrity, however twisted, they must have. And, too, they must be loners. They can have a partner, though only as a secondary figure. She, as in the case of Lisa Cody's Anna Lee, can have a boss. But essentially, because of the knight-errant image underneath, the private-eye must walk alone.

Partly because of this hidden knight-errantry you will need to make your private-eye, if you can, more of a person with whom your reader can identify. The private-eye, as it were, drives two-fisted into the story. He or she *is* your story. So you will want your reader to ride very closely on their shoulder.

How to achieve this? By remembering it, and by willing it. The possibility of close identification will come to the reader as a series of tiny hints, the way your hero looks at what comes before him or her, the exact tone in which they answer the people they meet. Out of these minute indications, which can only be put on the page as a result of a firmly held original image, comes that necessary close sympathy.

Because your story is told actively, through the places your private-eye goes to and the people he or she encounters, you will need to have much less of the puzzle element than was needed by the writers of detective stories and even the writers of detective novels. Of course, you will have to have one single underlying tug, just as the classical writers had their who-dun-it tug. And, in all probability, your tug will be much the same as theirs. Someone will have been murdered, and the reader, like your private-eye, will want to know whose hand held the gun. But because these books are written with a greater apparent degree of realism, the murder does not need to be the attention-grabbing, bizarre affair of the blueprint book.

You will probably need, as in the blueprint story, some clues as well. Your reader will be more interested in going in two-fisted with your hero than in observing the discarded paper bag smelling of oranges in the waste-paper basket. (It was used to make a 'gun shot' by being popped at the right moment, thereby creating the wrong time for the murder. Thank you, Dame Agatha.) But your readers will still get some satisfaction in the end from hearing what the detective deduced from something that was put before their own eyes and which they passed over.

There is a nice example of this in what is perhaps the classic private-eye story of them all. Dashiell Hammett's *The Maltese Falcon*. You will remember (if you don't, get hold of the book this minute) that Sam Spade's partner, Archer, is shot dead early in the story. Sam is summoned by a friend in the Police Department to see the body before it is taken away. He looks at a wooden fence, a section of which was ripped away when the dead man fell back with the bullet in his heart, and he suggests what must have happened. His Police Department friend agrees. 'That's it,' Tom replied slowly, working his brows together. 'The blast burnt his coat.' Then Sam asks at once who found the body. And there, in exactly the manner I have recommended for putting in clues in the traditional whodunit, Hammett gives his readers their clue, full-out and in the open but made to look as if it was there as part of the particularly laconic, cool conversation the two men are having over the newly-slain body. The clue is, of course, that if Archer's coat was powder-stained his killer must have been someone known to him who could get up that close in the deserted night street where he met his end.

The scrap of Hammett's dialogue I have quoted serves to show us one more necessary, if not absolutely necessary, ingredient of the private-eye novel, the use of racy, everyday speech. Such dialogue reinforces that world-seen-from-just-underneath atmosphere which is an aspect of the crusading image of the private-eye. Indeed, even your narration will need to take on a more direct tone. Partly this is so as not to contrast too blatantly with the speech patterns of your characters. Partly it is to give you that extra pace which the active, probing, investigating story requires.

Because—no harm in saying it once again—this is the essence of the private-eye novel: that the hero actively goes out and grabs the facts. Your detective of the detective story, of course, went about seeking information. But he acquired it as an onlooker. The private-eye seizes it as a participator. One great advantage of this is that you can afford to have many more scenes in which your hero questions suspects or witnesses. We have seen that in the detective story and even in the detective novel, scenes such as this used too often risk boredom in the reader. They have a similarity about them, and a slowness. But in the private-eye story such scenes become not gentle probings but confrontations. They have in-built drama.

You can safely let your hero move from one person to another fiercely demanding what they need to know. You have to remember only that from each such encounter he must, to make the story one of continuing progress and placate Thomas Ozro MacAdoo, take some new fact, something that leads them on, in most cases, to another confrontation—and takes us, the readers, with them.

A final note. When I originally wrote this book, in 1986, I felt happy to use 'he' for the private-eyes I was talking about. But since then what amounts to a new sub-genre in crime fiction has arisen. The female private-eye novel. It has its own rules, and its own considerable successes, as appealing to male readers as to women. Here are some of the rules for the female private-eye novel:

- the Investigator must be, of course, female but also positive, even sparky (so Miss Marple, fine though she is) doesn't qualify

- the Investigator may tackle any crime of any sort but it must be under her own steam, i.e. she must be the incontrovertible hero (NOT heroine) and have help only from such experts as she chooses to ask (this includes boy-friends and husbands)

- the Investigator shall be tough, but still retain a feminine compassion

- two rules that seem to have emerged, but which as a male enjoyer of the sub-genre I could wish never had: a) the Investigator should be ecologically minded, b) she should spend some part of the book either out running or in the gym.

To gain further insight into these rules you can do no better than read the novels of Sue Grafton, Sara Paretsky and the Carlotta Carlyle stories of Linda Barnes, or with an English setting Liza Cody, already mentioned, or Sarah Lacey.

Police procedurals

The huge lateral leap taken when, by reaction to the classical detective story and its immediate heirs, the private-eye tale came into being was not the only major change in the history of crime fiction since Edgar Allan Poe. One other sideways bound was the creation of what has come to be called the police procedural. This, as its name indicates, is crime fiction based fundamentally on actual police investigation of a crime, usually murder, for the same old reason that murder signals to the reader that the book carries a certain weight. Because police procedurals, though they tend to have from the nature of their subject matter rather more social content than the straight murder puzzle, are still books written primarily as entertainment.

They invite the reader to consider what police work is, how necessary it is for society today and even on occasion how, paradoxically, certain sorts of 'good' police work can bring about evil. But they do this within the limits of the novel of entertainment. If a writer produces a novel in which the role of the police in society outweighs all other considerations, then what has been produced is precisely a novel and not a work of crime fiction.

Curiously, this branch of crime fiction appears to have sprung up independently on either side of the Atlantic at much the same time. Where exactly it began rather depends on whether or not you decide to categorise certain books as police procedurals or as perhaps crime novels. For instance, in 1940 a British author of fairly conventional detective stories, Henry Wade (who was in private life Sir Henry

Aubrey Fletcher, a magistrate and son of a full-time Metropolitan magistrate, and thus not unacquainted with police work) wrote a book called *The Lonely Magdalen*, telling the story of a murder investigation seen largely from the point of view of the police officers conducting it. Meanwhile, in America in 1945 an author called Lawrence Treat, who had half-a-dozen crime books already under his belt, produced one called *V as in Victim*, which did much what *The Lonely Magdalen* had done. Later Treat, who followed *V as in Victim* with other books in the same vein, was to say, 'I didn't know I was writing police procedurals until somebody invented the term and said that was the kind of thing I was writing.'

He had no direct followers, however. Neither did Henry Wade in Britain. So in 1950 the American, Hillary Waugh, impressed by a volume of real murder cases he had picked up, not so much because of the horrific details the author had dwelt on as by the tone of authenticity that seemed to arise naturally from the accounts of the cases, decided to write a fictional crime story catching as much as he could of this real-life feel. The result, published in 1952, was a book called *Last Seen Wearing*, and it definitively established the police procedural in America.

In Britain that extraordinarily prolific crime author, John Creasey (more than 600 titles; 25 pseudonyms), was challenged one day by a police inspector neighbour to 'show us as we are'. Under the name of J. J. Marric he then produced from 1955 onwards a series of books written round a police officer by the name of Gideon. These, too, had their imitators and thus established the police procedural in Britain.

In the States the classic examples, which you should study, are the books of Ed McBain about the work of the detectives of the '87th Precinct' in an unnamed city. In Britain you could not do better than to pick out from the varied products of the author John Wainwright, an ex-policeman, those of his books that are in the police procedural mode or to look out for the books of two other policeman-writers, Graham Ison and Keith Wright. From each author you can learn how the police procedural should be put together. From each you can get a good idea of what police work in the respective countries is really like.

John Wainwright often calls police work 'bobbying'. And bobbying and what it means, if you have your eye on writing this sort of book, is what you will first have to absorb to the very marrow of your bones. But, you say, oughtn't I to be a policeman or a former policeman myself, like John Wainwright, to be able to do this? No, what you have got to be, like John Wainwright, is a writer. One of the absolutely necessary qualities of any writer of fiction is the possession of what is called empathy, the ability to see life through the eyes of people very different from oneself. If you have this, or succeed in cultivating it, then you will write better police procedurals than any policeman, however versed in his trade, who does not possess the quality.

Perhaps the very first thing you will discover in acquiring a knowledge of actual police work, though it is in fact obvious, is that the sort of murders the police deal with are very different from the sort of murders that the detectives of detective stories dealt with. With the latter, each case, each murder, was a duel with a murderer who, of necessity, had to be almost as brilliantly clever as they were themselves. However, even those murders in real life that rise above the simple snatching up of the kitchen knife in the middle of a husband and wife row are much less cunningly contrived than that.

So the sort of murder you will have in your police procedural will present virtually no challenge to the reader to guess or work out who-dun-it before your detectives. Some element of mystery, of course, will remain. But it will scarcely be more, nor need it be more, than the mere fact of no name being able to be clearly attached to the murderer till the book is nearly over. Yet one remnant from that classical template must still be there: your reader will be disappointed if the murderer has not been 'seen' at an early stage in the book, however unlike real life that may be.

I have said that in the classical version each murder was a duel between two giants. Now, in the more nearly real world of the police procedural, things will be very different. Murders in real life are not solved by one man, genius or not, working alone. So you are very unlikely to be able to tell your story (and, once again, telling a story is what you are doing fundamentally) without abandoning more than once the angel-on-the-shoulder viewpoint of whatever chief character you have chosen. You will probably have to see events through the eyes of one or more detectives, of a scene-of-the-crime officer, of various laboratory experts and of the man who sits in his office at headquarters and directs the operation. So gone is that staple of the detective story and its heirs as well as of the private-eye story, the loner.

With the loner's departure goes, too, the amateur detective's ability to disregard the law on occasion, and that of the private-eye. Your investigators now will not only have to keep to the law but they will have to obey regulations as well, or only occasionally and with their eye very much over their shoulder slide past them. It is cramping for the author, but if you have contracted with your readers to tell them, through a story, what police work is really like then you must accept this limitation.

So, without a Great Detective, or even a lesser detective of the fictional breed, you will find that the clearing up of the mystery, which still must be presented with an air of progress, will be carried out not largely by the processes of ratiocination (that word invented by Edgar Allan Poe) but by the duller process of the accumulation of facts, as in real life.

Almost all the murders that the police solve in real life are either dealt with in a matter of hours (the husband done it with the kitchen knife) or as the result of long, long, tedious inquiries, mostly house-to-house, the taking of fingerprints and the elimination of perhaps thousands of marginal suspects. 'Policemen,' once wrote the author Michael Gilbert, whose police procedurals you would do well to read as well as his other crime stories, 'did not catch murderers by taking thought. They caught them by taking statements.'

But the recounting of all the statements a team of detectives might take in the course of a major inquiry is hardly going to make you a book that will grip readers. No, for all the realism that is necessary in the police procedural, in the end you have to fake things. As, of course, all novelists, however wedded they are to the idea of realism, have to do. You select the facts that are telling (pun intended), the facts that will advance your story or make clear your characters or even make your locations easy to assimilate, and you hope that from them you can produce something that is not too far distant from the unwritable reality. A police procedural probably has more realism in it than any other kind of crime fiction, but at some point you have to ask your readers, as elsewhere, to suspend disbelief. And you have to 'ask' them by sheer, skilful, onward-moving writing.

So the writer of police procedurals is basically faced with the task of making what is in life dull, into reading that is as far as possible exciting. How can you do it?

The answer, which may seem not to be immediately helpful, is by the power of your pen. I have already instanced the first chapter of Simenon's *Maigret's Pickpocket*, which consists of no more than a description of Maigret riding to work on a bus, as being as gripping as any chase sequence, from the absolute accuracy of the writing and its complete economy. But if you are less than a writer of near genius, can you by simply describing what your policemen do, hold your readers spellbound?

Well, you can probably go some of the way by concentrating on the humanity of the policemen you need to portray. Having decided what it is in your story that they will have to do, try to switch to thinking of each one of them as a simple human being. Put yourself as much as you can into their shoes. Think with them. Feel with them. Make them real people.

In doing this you will probably find that you have become concerned, not simply with the particular task they have to carry out, but with their relations with other officers carrying out other tasks or involved with other aspects of the investigation you are writing about, even down to such matters of internal etiquette as how high does an officer have to rank before he can go into the office of a superior without knocking? (Something written of, quite fascinatingly, in one of John Creasey's Gideon books.) Such considerations are the life blood of the police procedural.

As are considerations that go a step beyond them, such as a policeman's attitude to his wife and family (he is stopped from going off duty at the time his wife expects: what will be her reaction?) or an unmarried policeman's love life, or for that matter the love life of a policeman who is cheating on his wife. Any of these factors may well interact with the investigation you have caught him up in, and they thus become an integral part of your book.

Let me add, though, a word of warning: scenes such as these must be just that, an integral part of your story. If you simply switch from writing about an investigation over which you have enlisted your reader's sympathy to scenes of home life or love life that have no connection with the main story, you will lose each time a little of your hold on the reader.

One side advantage of using these human interest aspects of the police procedural is that here at least you will have to do no research, or no more than is required by looking into your own heart. But for all those aspects of your book that arise directly from police activity you will indeed have to find out what are the real-life facts. Here you are in an altogether different situation from Ruth Rendell writing her crime novels and saying cheerfully that she avoids errors in describing police work 'by leaving it out'. Here you must know and use the real facts of police work.

How can you do this? One answer, and a good one, I have already suggested: by reading the books of acknowledged masters of the police procedural. But perhaps I should add one word of warning: look in the front of such books for the date of publication, be careful if they are at all old. Police procedures change, and even police attitudes change over the years. So if, for instance, you are reading the earliest Gideon books of John Creasey, stop at each fact that you feel inclined to take unto yourself and ask whether it is a reasonably timeless fact, or only a temporary one.

Perhaps this is the place to digress a little and talk about the taking of facts from other writers' books. Is it something you should do, or do you lay yourself open to terrible legal procedings? The answer is, in theory, clear—and in French. The words of the great dramatist, Moliére: *je prends mon bien où je le trouve.* I take my goodies from wherever I find them. In other words what any other writer has written is open territory. But what you must *not* do (and could conceivably lay yourself open to legal proceedings by doing) is to quote exactly and at some length. This is plagiarism. But to take some fact that a novelist has written of and to add it to the mishmash at the back of your mind and then to reproduce it as part of the web you eventually weave: this is the process of creation. It only remains to add that there is—damn it—a thin grey area between the two.

But to revert to the subject of getting information about police work, the next most accessible source after the books of the police procedural writers is, of course, television. Many of the police series go to great lengths to ensure an authentic feel (otherwise the companies get shoals of complaints from the policemen who avidly watch such shows, and sometimes begin to model their behaviour on what they see). So you can safely pick up a good deal of useful stuff here. Only, once again, be alert. Not every police series intends to be authentic. However, it is generally easy enough to sort out the ones that do and the ones that aim to provide police-based fantasy.

Non-fiction books, too, it goes without saying, are a good source. You can go to your local library and consult the section concerned with 'Police' and see what's there. Once again, though, be wary of the out-of-date.

Finally, you can go to the horse's mouth. Even if you are not lucky enough to have, as John Creasey did, a police officer as a neighbour or fellow member of some institution, you are likely to find on the whole that a visit to your local police station will pay off. After all, it is flattering to a hard-working policeman to think that someone as glamorous, or glamorous-seeming, as an author wants to know about his dull daily life. And I myself have found the Press Office at New Scotland Yard reasonably helpful at the end of the telephone.

All of these sources will, besides supplying you with specific points you may want to know about, help you to shift your viewpoint. If up to now you have thought of crime fiction in the traditional way, with a detective hero, with an attention-grabbing murder, you have now got to look on the art from quite a different angle. You have got to accustom yourself to the book that is written from several different viewpoints.

You may even want to produce the sort of book that is popular in America, the police procedural concerned with as many as half a dozen different crimes investigated by as many officers linked to each other only by working out of the same squad room. The books of Elizabeth Linington, Dell Shannon and Lesley Egan (she is all one and the same person) are good examples. Personally, I find them less absorbing than the book that contrives to tell only one story, with as many ramifications as may be. But there are not a few readers for such procedurals and you may feel that writing one of them is what you can do best.

Yet if you are telling a story you will very likely need to have, not a hero through whose eyes all is seen, but at least one fairly central figure with whom your readers can chiefly identify.

But he, or she, now will no longer be the sole fighter against whatever criminal lurks in the shadows. He will be just one detective working among a whole complex of colleagues. And, more, he will have to be, since the realities are what we are trying to portray, a person of ordinary talents and weaknesses. Nor will he, in the tradition of the detective hero of old, keep the meaning of any discoveries to himself. The police procedural has no room for the Holmes-Watson set-up. So the solving of your mystery should be a much more gradual affair than any sudden flash of revelation coming to the hero and being kept under his deerstalker till almost the last page.

One final constriction. You will almost inevitably find, as you begin to think what sort of a story your police procedural might have, that it will have to be set in a city of some size. The reason is simple. If your book is a success, you will want to write others with the same setting. But in all places save the bigger cities murder is a rare event, and had you chosen some small locality, however well known to you and attractive, your atmosphere of realism would be reduced every time that one more murder (and murder you almost must have) was notified to the police station.

The suspense novel

There is one other major kind of crime fiction open to the writer of today which we must look at. It is the suspense novel, a type more easily recognised than defined. The suspense novel stops short of the pure thriller, a kind of writing that falls outside the scope of this book, but it is not always easy to say just where the line should be drawn. The best I can manage is to say that the thriller is intended to thrill; it is a succession of exciting events, whereas the suspense novel is designed to create suspense, a series of situations of which the outcome is in doubt.

From this we can go on to discover one of the rules for this sort of crime fiction. Although a suspense novel consists of that series of situations with doubtful outcomes, the final outcome is not, paradoxically, ever really in doubt. The hero or heroine must ultimately come out on top. This is what the reader expects, and if you want to write a book in which this unequivocally does not happen then you probably want to write a straight novel, so off you go and don't bother us any more.

I say 'a book in which this unequivocally does not happen' because the happy ending which the reader insists on does not need by any means to be a simple, pure, unalloyed happy ending. If you have succeeded in fully engaging the sympathies of your readers you will probably have produced for them a main character who is something more than a stereotype, who has about him or her a good deal of the complexity of real life. So a mixed ending, part loss, part that essential gain, will arise almost naturally.

You will see from the ground rules I have attempted to give that the suspense novel, as much as the crime novel, is an amorphous thing. It may well cut across two, three or four of the neat categories we have already discussed. Indeed, the only real way one can pinpoint it is by saying that in it the notion of suspense, of repeated and ever-growing suspense, predominates.

The writer who feels that suspense is best suited to his or her talents would do well before setting out, however, to get it clear in his or her own head that suspense is what is to be produced and that the book contemplated will adopt this form, or formula, in preference to any other. Then readers will get the satisfaction they have been led to expect. It is as well to be clear in this way that you are giving priority to suspense because, of course, there are elements of suspense not only in almost all crime fiction but in almost all fiction of any sort. (Will Darcy marry Elizabeth Bennet?)

So the key to writing the suspense story is the creation, one after another, of situations of suspense. And needless now perhaps to say, such situations should mount up on a progressive scale so that they make an ongoing story. This is not something always easy to achieve. But it is probably good advice to plan this sort of book every bit as much as the writer of the puzzle detective story will have had to work out the plot and most of what is necessary to sustain that plot. The temptation with the suspense novel, a book in which a high degree of identification both from intellectual curiosity and emotional involvement is necessary for the writer as much as the reader, is to catch hold of some intriguing initial situation, sit down at the word-processor and go racing ahead from there.

It can be done. For some writers this is the only way. But it is risky. You lay yourself open to producing, instead of a series of ascending suspense moments, a series of descending ones at worst, or of switchbacking ones with readers losing interest with each less gripping situation. So, if you can, plan ahead in rough outline.

This is not to say that whatever mystery you have chosen so as to lead your hero or heroine into these successively more and more suspenseful situations will have to be kept entirely hidden from your reader till the last pages. No, the suspense novel does inherit from the traditional detective story that element of mystery (though this need not involve a murder and the mystery of who committed it) but it does not at all inherit the need to have a battle of wits with the reader. Once the mystery has provided a sufficient reason for hero or heroine to find themselves in a good opening situation of suspense, the person or persons behind that mystery can be safely revealed.

From then on the pattern of the book becomes, not a search, but a struggle. It will be a struggle between your hero and whatever associates he may have and the forces of evil opposed to him. Read, for a splendid example of this, any of the books of Dick Francis. With all the sense of timing learnt as a champion jockey, he creates situation after situation of rising suspense to hold readers by the hundred thousand glued to the battle of wits between hero and villains that he has devised.

But if the physical violence that Dick Francis writes of so well, without glorying in it, without dismissing it in the way cruder writers do as they allow a hero to leap into action after some terrible beating-up, if this does not fire your imagination you can still write suspense novels that will satisfy readers every bit as well.

Suspense does not need to be created by violence or even by the threat of explicit violence. It can be created by a feeling of mere unrealised menace. To see how this is done by experts, read some of the British novels of Celia Fremlin or the American novels of Ursula Curtiss. The smallest unexplained happenings can give a hero or heroine the feeling that something terrible is about to occur.

Of course, to write this sort of book you will need to be able to put yourself into such a central character's mind. But if the idea of some indefinable menace frees your imagination, then there is nothing to stop you producing a suspense novel every bit as twanging with tension as a story in which someone is left hanging by one finger over a depthless gorge.

The same rules apply. You must develop a series of ever more suspenseful situations and, though your hero or heroine must eventually 'be all right', the final denouement must not be a let-down. 'It was all a dream' is the worst possible ending to a story of a nightmare by day. But your suspenseful situations do not necessarily ever need to become other than subtle. You should keep in mind the phrase 'an undertone of unease' and aim for that. And if you want to watch a master of this sort of book at work, read the later novels of the American, Margaret Millar.

You can create suspense out of subtlety. But equally you can create suspense out of going to the very edge. One of the best ways of getting to the heart of a character is to put him or her into a situation of extreme testingness. If this notion suits you temperamentally, then try producing this sort of suspense novel. What you will need fundamentally is to hit on some situation that puts the greatest stress imaginable on a person not too dissimilar from yourself or from the majority of your readers.

Taking an iron-clad hero and facing him with some massive task will not produce that air of almost unbearable suspense you should be looking for. It will produce, in all probability, an adventure novel or thriller, something perfectly good in its own terms but not what we are concerned with here. For some classic examples of almost unbearable tension read the novels of the late Francis Clifford.

For a different strand of suspense, also brought about by going to the very edge, read the novels of Patricia Highsmith. She is a writer, not delighted in by everybody, who plainly finds what fires her imagination is considering people who go beyond the ordinary bounds. Indeed she has spoken admiringly of criminals who are 'active, free in spirit, and do not knuckle down to anyone'. And the hero of a number of her books is one Tom Ripley, several times murderer, who is always allowed to get away with it. You can see why everyone is not a Highsmith fan, and perhaps why some of us are impassioned ones.

But by taking such extreme cases Patricia Highsmith is enabled to say something, a great deal even, about our world as it is. And she does this by telling the stories of her different heroes in a series of ever more tense situations of suspense, situations where the outcome is fearfully doubtful. We are far here from the classical detective story for the hero detective has been replaced by the hero murderer. But if you, too, see life through such dark spectacles, perhaps a book with a murderer hero, with whom your readers are going to sympathise if you can possibly make them (notice how in the later Ripley book Patricia Highsmith shows him as a loving gardener) or with any other sort of anti-law hero, this is the sort of work you should be addressing yourself to. I would not like to have to make a ruling over any Highsmith novel as to whether it is a crime novel or a suspense novel but, whichever it is, it shows what can be done at the frontiers of crime fiction.

4
On the Periphery

There remain a few kinds of crime fiction we have yet to look at. These are, if you like, minor branches at the outer edge of the great tree. But one of them may be the sort of book you feel you are best fitted to write. They are comic crime and its cousin, farce crime; romantic suspense; historical crime and its near relation, crime set in the immediate past; and finally, the crime short story.

Comic crime

Crime and the comic: at first glance the two seem almost exact opposites. But anyone who has read more than a little crime fiction will know that in fact the two often go together. Crime fiction comes, you can say, in two modes. There is the black face of violence and there are the spreading hips of cosiness. It is with the latter sort of crime fiction that those of us who enjoy writing comedy will have most to do. On the whole, if we choose this sort of writing, we will be acknowledging that our aim is not of the highest. But if we provide readers with amusement when things are glum we are performing at the least a useful service.

'If one is basically more anxious to please and amuse people than to keep an implacably appraising eye on them,' the author of the urbane and chucklingly funny Appleby books, Michael Innes, has said, 'one will never take the first step towards considerable writing.' But one will have taken the first step, and the second and the third, towards providing readers with pleasant entertainment.

Of course, some humour can also be used in those books that do keep something of an implacable eye on people. Humour can provide passages of necessary relaxation in stories where it is otherwise inappropriate. This is what we might call the Porter Scene in Macbeth technique. But its use is not by any means the main function of the books in which it may be necessary, and there is little to be said about it. A scene of high tension can be greatly enhanced if it is preceded by a passage of comedy, as Shakespeare in preparing for Macbeth's murder of Duncan well knew. But the only other guidance necessary is to say: be as funny as it is in you to be but be careful not to go too far. Contrast with the grim event to come is what is wanted. It should be a seesaw affair. Putting too heavy a comedian on one end ruins the balance.

A similar comment also applies to the other sort of humour found in some basically unhumorous crime fiction; the wisecracks or one-liners in many private-eye stories and some other books. They are not a necessary ingredient. You will find few, if any, in the Brandstetter novels of Joseph Hansen, excellent though they are. Chandler, on the other hand, used them and delighted in them, and because of this a tradition has grown up that they should appear in every private-eye tale. Not so. But if you can produce them and like to do it, and if they fit the particular sort of book you are writing, well and good.

But we are concerned here with books in which the jokes are, more or less, the whole of the matter, inextricably bound up with the story that is being told. So perhaps the first thing to say is that, as with the story, there is a considerable art to the pacing of humour.

Not only should your jokes and humorous episodes be relevant to the theme of your book (however slight that might be), but you should remember that a good joke becomes less good if it is followed too closely by another good joke. And each of them becomes less and less funny if they are too closely followed by a third. But how close is close? I wish I could give you a simple straightforward answer, like 'Each joke should be separated from the one before it by at least 1050 words'. Of course, I can't. Timing is something that has to be felt.

Curiously, perhaps the only advice to be given is: cultivate it in any field you like, in sport, in dancing, in singing, in telling dirty stories, and what you learn there will mysteriously invade any other field in which timing is important, unless some mental block prevents it. And this includes writing crime fiction in general, and humorous crime fiction in particular.

The second thing to say about humorous crime fiction is

that you have to reconcile in your pages that sharp difference between crime, which arises from evil, and laughter, which is by and large a manifestation of good. Although you will be writing a story in which a murder, or more than one murder, is the key happening, you have got to make it compatible with the humour with which you intend to infuse the whole.

The way to do it is to treat that murder in as formal a manner as you can. The classical way Agatha Christie (who did not on the whole write humorous crime stories) managed this often will give you an idea of what to aim for. She would have her victim murdered, unless the plot demanded otherwise, by a 'neat hole in the middle of the forehead'. Never mind that this is very seldom what happens when a bullet strikes a forehead and especially when it comes out at the back of the head. Writing of murder thus, in a thoroughly formal way, you can successfully establish two different things: that a murder has taken place and in consequence the story you are telling must be looked on as being of some weight, and that nothing has happened to arouse any revulsion in your readers.

This will do very well for the sort of story that is a combination of the novel of humour (a story of cumulative comic events) and the blueprint detective story. But there is another type of comic crime fiction that is open to you, and in which the formula we have talked about will need some adjustment. This is the detective novel or the crime novel which makes its comments on life through humour rather than more directly. A fine example is Julian Symons' novel *The Man Who Lost His Wife*, or from America the excellent *Handling Sin* by Michael Malone and the rather jokier and somewhat less deep novels of Carl Hiaasen.

If you have it in you to comment on our times through humour, generally of the deflationary sort, then combining this with a crime story may bring you extra dividends. The crime element will provide your readers with a greater incentive to turn the pages than the mere wish to see what comic event will happen next. So your plot needs to be a reasonably strong one. You will need the who-dun-it tug more than in some other forms of crime fiction, and the murder situation in which you have involved the hero of your comic novel ought to be a serious one, otherwise the whole enterprise will seem merely frivolous and you will risk readers dropping out.

But the who-dun-it tug is not the only resource you have in writing comic crime fiction. In this sort of book you may well find that the pattern of how-will-he-get-out-of-this is more convenient to use while underneath you get on with the purpose of your story. A succession of situations, each one more impossible than the last, may be what will best serve you.

In this sort of book your hero will be something of an ordinary individual, a person with whom your readers can easily sympathise. He or she will be someone to whom, owing to the quite serious situation they have become involved in, events of a comic, deflationary character happen.

But in another variety of comic crime fiction you can take as a chief character, as indeed your detective, a person who is to a greater or lesser extent a figure of fun, someone prone to fall victim to more or less ridiculous circumstances. I suppose the classic example comes not from a book but from the world of film, Inspector Clouseau as portrayed by Peter Sellers. But the character in the film ceases to amuse when presented on the printed page. Somehow it does not seem to matter in the fast-moving, no-going-back whirl of a film that the hero is a complete fool. In a book it does matter. A reader is more involved than a film-goer. Sympathies are more aroused. So a complete fool will not acquire a following.

So what you must do, and it is not easy, is to create a clown-like detective hero who has a core of toughness, of shrewdness even, which will allow him in the end plausibly to come out on top. Because the old rule still applies; in the detective story or the detective novel in the end there must be triumph, although that triumph may be flawed.

It is a question of striking a balance between the amount of vulnerable, comic, accident-prone quality you allow in your detective and the sort of book you want to write. If you are aiming almost for pure comedy, then your detective will need only the smallest core of toughness or commonsense. An example you would do well to learn from, if this sort of book appeals to you as a potential writer, is the laugh-a-line Angel books of Mike Ripley.

On the other hand, you may want to write a book in which the element of comedy is much less strong. Then your detective should have much more of the qualities that make for success in a real police officer, and much less vulnerability to comic events. I offer as an example some of my own Inspector Ghote novels, particularly the early ones, since I have found it possible in recent years to shift, as it were, Ghote's character into higher, more serious gear.

Just as your detective, however comic, needs a basis of solid fact, so does a story set in the comic mode. The more securely you can establish a base of reality before your comic events start their upwards spiral, the more willing will your readers be to accept happenings that on the face of them are unlikely and ridiculous.

The same applies to character. The more solidly rooted your characters are as being people like oneself or one's readers, the more willing will those readers be to countenance absurd events happening to them. And the funnier those absurd events will seem.

Farce crime

Absurd events. This brings us from considering comic crime fiction to considering an even trickier form, farce crime. Read as an example the books of Joyce Porter featuring the gross, lazy and self-indulgent Inspector Dover, if you can find them; the last was published in 1980. They take on this difficult combination of crime (which is, after all, a serious matter almost all of the time) but advance it into the field of farce.

But the author I would particularly recommend if farce crime fiction attracts you is Colin Watson, with his stories of life in the imaginary provincial town of Flaxborough. Colin Watson had a great talent for farce writing. He was able to take characters who at the start seemed ordinary enough, if prone to human weaknesses and vices, and to elevate them into the world of the scarcely real, of adventures and encounters riddled with the absurd. And it was as crime stories, mystery puzzles, that he chose to embody his way of commenting on the follies of mankind.

Judgment of humorous writing is even more subjective than with any other kind. What makes me laugh won't necessarily make you laugh. But, to my mind, Colin Watson brings off almost every time the difficult feat he attempts. Again, he does it by starting with both feet firmly on the ground. His provincial town of Flaxborough is a portrait of what might be any somewhat cut-off provincial town anywhere in Britain. It is rooted in reality.

Then too, Colin Watson was particularly adept in the

creation of the detective he chose to investigate, or struggle with, the curious crimes he made to happen in everyday Flaxborough. His Inspector Purbright is a very ordinary man, distinguished only perhaps by the mildly quizzical view of life and humanity he possesses. But through his eyes Watson was enabled to describe events of the utmost absurdity in a way that makes you believe, if only while you are in thrall to each book, that they really *might* have happened.

So, if this way of looking at the world is what starts up that vital fire in your imagination, then you would do well to take Watson's tip and have as your hero someone imbued with plenty of ordinary commonsense. Then you can gradually give way to your instinct for describing the purely ridiculous event that can seem extraordinarily funny.

For examples of this way of writing seen in the American manner, that is, told with that tremendous briskness of pace and with a fine spattering of one-line wisecracks, let me recommend the farce crime novels of Donald E. Westlake. In them you will see in the hands of a master (though not every book he writes is farce crime) how to achieve that build-up of ever more ridiculous events that is the key to success in this form of crime fiction.

They well illustrate a quality which is perhaps more necessary in farce crime fiction than in any other branch of the art, the need to set up a cracking pace. If you are going to try to convince a reader that something wildly unlikely has taken place then one useful tool at your command is to produce a story that sweeps the reader along from incident to incident in a headlong tumble.

They illustrate, too, another talent you will need, or need to cultivate: deftness. You are likely to have some ticklish moments, times when perhaps corpse clashes with comedy. Then you will need all your feeling for words, all your resources of vocabulary, to get yourself neatly out of trouble.

You will need, too, on a broader scale to be deft in matching your plot with the general style you have chosen to work in. If you are going to be lightly humorous, skimming like a butterfly, then you will be ill served by a plot that is impossibly ingenious or a plot that has at its centre something too grave to be dealt with light-heartedly when, long after you have embarked on the actual writing, the moment comes to reveal all.

So a final piece of advice. If you feel you have a gift for

humour and have decided to combine it with crime, which is an excellent thing to do if you have the skill, then be careful not to let that humour run away with you. It is all too easy (I speak from experience) when you hit on a sequence of events that seems funny, to get the bit between your teeth and run on and on.

What you write may well be funny, but if it had grown to the extent where it overweighs the actual book you are writing, a piece of comic crime fiction, then you will be spoiling the whole. As your readers read they may be delighted with what you are doing, but when they reach the end of your book they will be less pleased with the whole rather than they might have been. They will be less inclined to read your next.

Romantic suspense

Very different from comic crime fiction and farce crime is a yet more popular branch of the art, romantic suspense fiction, otherwise known as gothic fiction. No laughs here: they are fatal to the atmosphere it is necessary to build up. This type of book may be said to ante-date the classical detective story, which we have called the template or original of most crime fiction.

The pure gothic novel can safely be said to have started with Horace Walpole, the rich and eccentric son of the first Prime Minister of England. He built himself an extraordinary turrety and battlemented house, Strawberry Hill, at Twickenham in Middlesex, and then he wrote a romance, *The Castle of Otranto*, more or less using the house as a background. This is one book I don't advise you to read. Frankly, it's silly. But it was enormously popular when it first came out in 1764, and it started a whole train of similar books which even came to include such works of genius as the Brontë sisters' *Jane Eyre* and *Wuthering Heights*.

Into that stream of pure gothic fiction there was eventually added the element of crime or suspected crime, thus bringing into existence the romantic suspense novel. Though its popularity goes up and down a little according to the fashion of the year, the genre is plainly here to stay. It is a type of book open to any would-be-writer who feels he or she can work in the vein.

I must put particular emphasis on 'she' because, of course, most books in this style are written by women, although by no means all. The emphasis should be on the feminine for another, and more important, reason. Romantic suspense is what might be called the literature of the night side of human experience. Or, to adopt a more scientific expression, the literature of the right-hand side of the brain. The left-hand side of the brain, so we are told, controls our rational, logical thinking; the right-hand side provides the intuitive. Of course, all human beings, male and female, have their share of each, but it seems that in many women the right-hand side, intuitive approach is more developed.

So, in one of the most notable romantic suspense novels ever written, Mary Roberts Rinehart's *The Circular Staircase* (and that's one, though it dates from 1909, you could well read) the heroine, Rachel Innes, says of herself and the adventure she became involved in, 'Madness seized me.' In other words, she abandoned the rational and made discoveries.

Yet another reason for regarding romantic suspense as primarily a woman's art (though I enjoy reading them, and so do many other old male chauvinists) is that the archetypal situation they describe echoes the situation of women through the ages. Typically, the heroine is in some confined, duty-bound situation, just as in life many, many women still are. Then this heroine does something that might seem sheer foolishness. She opens some forbidden door in true Bluebeard's castle style, or she enters some forbidden or forbidding house, and eventually breaks free.

Thus, beneath what may seem to be pure escapist entertainment, there lies a deep psychological truth. And the author of romantic suspense does well to let that truth at least seep into her unconscious before setting out to write one of the books in the genre. Its underlying force will, without this necessarily being apparent, lend charge to the final product. Such books are, too, always in the form of a struggle between Good and Evil. And again, though this seems elementary it represents a deep truth, and the background knowledge of it will give the eventual manuscript extra power.

So, since these books are from the right-hand side of the brain, they rely heavily on mood and emotion. In writing, do not be afraid to let these dictate the way you go. From your unconscious there may rise ideas, characters, actions you never would have believed yourself capable of thinking of.

Use then, as you roughly plan your book, some locality which for you evokes a strong mood. Do not be afraid of the cliché here, the brooding house, the wild rocks and wind-swept moors. Written of with emotion they can still ring true. But they can, too, be given a contemporary gloss. For instance, one of the cleverest of today's romantic suspense writers, Jennie Melville, has used industrial archaeology, the romance of abandoned machinery, to fine effect.

But if the brooding house really does seem too much of a cliché to you, if it fails to set fire to your imagination, then there is an alternative. Where once it was sufficient of an adventure for a lone girl to enter the deserted mansion at the far end of the village, today the element of adventure, of venturing, can be plausibly obtained at the end of a plane flight. All the world's exotic locations are open to you. And, as I have already mentioned, it is not altogether necessary, if your mind is constructed that way, actually to visit your chosen locale. Inspector Ghote's India is there for you to send yourself, or your heroine.

Romantic suspense novels are escape novels. Readers have their expectations of them, and that they should present an escape from the dreary realities of life is one of the most important of these. It is a pleasure in itself, and it is also a psychological event. Many people, many women, lead restricted lives. As your heroine escapes from the ordinary into danger, they too can escape with her, be exhilarated with her. So, whether your novel is set in the most distant parts of the world or in dear old Cornwall, be careful to omit the dull details of everyday living. Your heroine need not eat (except by implication), unless she dines opposite her destined mate in surroundings of unusual luxury or picnics simply with him in breathtakingly romantic circumstances.

Some details of mundane things, however, are particularly necessary. You will be much concerned in writing this sort of book to secure the maximum identification from your readers with your heroine. So what she wears is of considerable importance, and you will need to describe her clothes in fair detail, though with as much economy in the writing as you can manage. And, since most of your readers will be women, you should also describe the clothes other characters wear and to a lesser extent the rooms in which they meet each other. But these descriptions should be confined to what the heroine sees after her adventure has begun, and in them you want to aim for reality without its customary tackiness.

In the same way, if the adventure your heroine becomes

embroiled in involves a corpse, as it is likely to do, then you must confine the police presence, symbol of the harsh realities, to the very minimum. Remember that what your reader wants is not all the facts that a real-life situation would involve but only what I call the 'fiction-facts', those pieces of information that are necessary not for the situation in the real world you might be describing but for the story you are telling. One small technical trick to aid you in keeping the police at bay, I add, is for your corpse to be supposed to be the result of an accident, often seeming such to everybody but your incurably inquisitive heroine.

Your incurably inquisitive heroine. It is time we looked at her in more detail.

She will, of course, be the absolute centre of your story. The reader must see everything through her eyes, and, as I have already said, it is vital that your reader identifies with her. So, while you may well have some trait or peculiarity about her that will give her a mark of distinction, this must be something that does not disqualify her from maximum general sympathy.

Thus she may be immensely wealthy, or desperately poor, since these are conditions in which almost all of us in our fantasies can see ourselves. But she must not have a wooden leg or a cast in her eye, since these are things most of us hope to escape. On the other hand she can have a slight limp or consider herself (note the words) plain, since the majority of women are not faultless beauties.

What she can also have, which might at first glance seem off-putting, is great expertise in some abstruse art or science, though this should never of course be an unpleasant one. A heroine who is a sewage engineer is hardly going to appeal to the escapist element in your readership, but a heroine who is a top designer of aero engines would be a definite asset. We all of us in our Walter Mitty moments are apt to design a world-beating aero engine. Yet pause. If you do give your heroine this skill you will have to some extent to prove to your readers that she has it. You will have to know something, or be prepared to find out something, about designing aero engines, no easy task. But there are unusual skills or occupations of which it is easier to acquire knowledge. You may have one such yourself. Or some odd skill may spark your imagination; making jewellery; deciphering codes; knowing about Indian miniature painting. Then it's off to the library, a detailed study of perhaps just one book and your heroine could be a sufficiently convincing expert.

Now see the story through her eyes, from her point of view. So there can be no question where that story should start. It may start with the first glimpse she gets of the man she is destined to love, or the man she believes wrongly that she is destined to love. More conveniently for you as the creator of her adventure, your start could be her arrival. Her arrival where? Anywhere your fancy has lit on; as an employee at a large and mysterious house; as a holiday-maker at a romantic yet possibly menace-filled location.

And she must have a name. Dorothy Eden one of the best and most successful writers of romantic suspense novels, used in her earlier days to start her whole book from a name she had chosen, or that had perhaps chosen her by striking a note from the wind-harp in her mind—Seraphine, Blandina, Hariot. Old tombstones provided her with that lit match to the powder trail of her imagination. Then, with the notion of what a girl with such a name must be like firm in her mind, she made this heroine of hers arrive somewhere and without delay put her into the first of a series of conflicts with, behind them, a gradually increasing aura of mystery.

Remember, too, from what we have already said, that these conflicts need to be in order of ascending difficulty. As the heroine triumphs in one, something yet more filled with trouble should await her. Onwards and upwards her conflicts should go until the final and worst one of all. This will be the one that, when it is resolved, will bring the book to an end. And that end you would do well to have had in mind from the very beginning. No need, or less need, to plan more of a book which is to be written out of the right-hand side of your brain, out of intuition.

It will probably be a good thing, depending finally on your own particular temperament, not to be able to see too much of the immediate future for your heroine. Then, if you have that necessary possession for any writer, luck, your subconscious will provide you with developments you never could have thought of in cold blood. And, because they will have arisen not out of planning but out of the story you are telling, almost certainly each new development will have that necessary quality of being a worse trouble for your heroine until the final calamity at the end.

But that end you ought to have had a firm, if not wholly

clear idea of from the earliest thought you gave to your story. It will, of course, be a happy end. But, if you can contrive it, it will be all the better for being a happy end that will not have been wholly obvious to your readers. Yes, your heroine will be united with her destined mate. But perhaps in a way that will be something of a surprise.

In this contriving to do the obvious thing in a way not altogether obvious will lie the difference between producing a run-of-the-mill story, which may well never see the light of day, and producing a story with that something extra. It is not easy. You may be lucky and that necessary little twist may be given to you by the workings of intuition. But you may have to think hard and long and reject many ideas that seemed promising before arriving at an ending to your book that is at once what everyone all along expected and what no one, or hardly anyone, thought would happen in that way.

The same consideration applies to the initial impetus for your story. Your heroine is going to have to plunge herself into some sort of danger. The reader who has bought your book has bought it on the understanding that this is what will happen. But she, or he, will be disappointed if your heroine simply plunges foolishly and thoughtlessly into some obvious danger when, with hardly any thought, some alternative line of action lies open to her.

Had I but known . . . These are words to avoid having to use, or to use with great caution. There is a little poem by Ogden Nash from which a couple of (long) lines sum up the danger excellently.

> Sometimes it is the Had I But Known what grim secret lurked beneath the smiling exterior I would never have set foot within the door;
>
> Sometimes the Had I But Known then what I know now, I could have saved at least three lives by revealing to the Inspector the conversation I heard through that fortuitous hole in the floor.

The words are almost worth committing to memory to serve as a warning light when you find yourself in danger of making use of a similar situation. And don't think that it isn't a temptation. A forewarning to the reader that something important and mysterious is about to happen is extremely useful. Mary Roberts Rinehart used it to excellent effect in *The Circular Staircase*. But that was in 1909 and she has had so many successors that the device now sticks out like a sore thumb and must be used only with the greatest care and deftness of touch.

There is one other almost essential ingredient of the romantic suspense story that can hardly be avoided and yet which perhaps presents difficulties to anyone whose interest is more in the human relationships that are the core of this kind of book than in physical action and violence, things which seem to belong more properly to the thriller. Yet you will hardly be able to produce a romantic suspense story without at least one such action passage, probably your final confrontation and equally probably taking the form of a chase.

So it is worth considering briefly here how to write a chase scene or a scene of action, something of course which comes in many other sorts of crime fiction. The first thing to note is that a chase should be built up in exactly the way you build up the whole of your book. It should be a mounting series of difficulties, only here the difficulties are not major confrontations but small incidents such as a foot caught in a briar root or a gate that has always been open now proving to be locked.

Let your imagination roam with your desperately running heroine firmly in the centre of your mind and then from the incidents that will (if you have a ration of luck) spring up, arrange them in order of difficulty, if your intuition has not done that already for you. This is easily said, and I recognise that warring against this ideal state of affairs will be the actual circumstances of your story. You may, to put it crudely, want to have your heroine trip over that briar root but have set your story in a desert of soft shifting sand. However, the aim is the thing to bear in mind: each check in the chase to be worse than the one before it.

Let me call in as assistant instructor none other than Mr Graham Greene, with the advice I have already mentioned from one of his books of autobiography. (More for your reading list since they contain plenty of direct writing about writing.) Remember his saying that when you are out to create excitement, cling on to keeping things simple. Never muffle that excitement with a character's reflections, by similes and metaphors. A subject, a verb and an object and perhaps some rhythm in the language you use, that is all.

So that is what you have to do. But it is not as easy as perhaps it sounds. Adjectives will creep in, if my own experience is anything to go by. Or you hit on what seems a marvellously telling simile and cannot bear to omit it. Yet you should be tough. Graham Greene knows best.

From action to its opposite, talk. Dialogue, most writers find, is easier than description. Once get your heroine into one of those confrontations that are going to make up the greater part of her adventure, once have her facing another person and the words will flow.

Perhaps, however, because of the charged emotional situations that the romantic suspense novel calls for, these verbal confrontations will tempt you to get carried away. Your heroine makes a pointed remark, the mysterious man she is face to face with comes back with something yet sharper, more menacing. You find your word-processor tapping out or your pencil scrawling a yet more thrusting reply from your heroine, one that surprises even you yourself. But stop. Is what she said advancing your story? Does it throw a light your story needs on to her character? If it does, all is well. But all too easily it may not. It may be the start of a long slide away from the story you have to tell and if you let that happen you will, however quick and exciting the dialogue, eventually threaten your reader's interest in the whole.

Because, remember, what you are doing is telling a story. It is a story in an atmosphere of suspense and romance but first and foremost it is a story and everything, descriptions of settings, action scenes, characters, intriguing background or intriguing interest in the heroine must be subordinated to that overriding need. The story.

Mystery with history

'Combining mystery with history': this was a phrase I invented (or perhaps inadvertently cribbed) for the blurb of the first novel I wrote under the pseudonym of Evelyn Hervey, *The Governess*, a story in which Miss Harriet Unwin in her first post as a governess in 1870s London finds herself accused of murder and has to pinpoint the real killer to save herself from the Old Bailey. In writing the book I was jumping on to something of a bandwagon. In recent years mystery with history has become a popular sub-genre of crime fiction.

Almost any period in history is open to you if the things that happened in the past set your imagination whirling. It is often stated that the detective story was an impossibility before there was an established order in society and a more than rudimentary police force to support it. This is true, of course, in so far as it means that no contemporary authors were going to write stories about a single murderer being exposed when lawlessness was rife and human life generally seen as of little account. But it does not mean that, with some ingenuity, you cannot set a detective story, or almost any of its variants and successors, at some period in the past.

Lindsey Davis, for example, has in a delightful series of books succeeded in combining the days of Ancient Rome with the chirpiness of the downbeat private-eye novel. While the novels of Anton Gill go back even further, to the 'cases' of the scribe Huy in Ancient Egypt, a setting once used too by Agatha Christie herself in *Death Comes As the End.*

Mystery with history novels fall, by and large, into the category of cosy crime as opposed to unsettling crime, and perhaps their increasing popularity is due in part to the increasing difficulty of writing the old-fashioned mystery in today's troubled times. Peter Lovesey, whose Victorian police procedural novels featuring Sergeant Cribb are fine examples of this branch of the art, has summed it up neatly in saying that he sees himself writing books that are a 'counterpoise of teacups and terror'. The terror, be it noted, all safely in the past.

Lovesey's books have been called by some critics pastiches, though he is firm in stating that he intended to produce the equivalent of the police procedural in the days when there was not much procedure and not all that many police. When the Metropolitan Police first introduced detective officers, as they were called, in 1842 (nominal strength: 2) many newspapers attacked the idea virulently. It was, they said, 'unEnglish' to spy on anybody, and *Punch* delighted for years afterwards to speak of the Defective Department.

So it would be as well to distinguish clearly in our minds between the historical crime book that is pastiche and the book that is an attempt to portray some distant time through a crime story. Both have their adherents, among writers and among readers. The latter sub-branch is self-explanatory. The former may need a word or two said about it.

Pastiche has been defined as a literary work that imitates the work of an earlier writer. But there is generally a little more to it than that. Pastiche is apt not simply to imitate but to imitate with exaggeration. It gently mocks. Well done, it is delightful. You pick out the chief traits of the book of yore or the time of yore you fancy and you bring these to the fore. But it is not easy to do this without becoming crude, and since the art appeals principally for its sensitiveness to what it is mocking, crudity has the effect of alienating those readers the pastiche should most attract.

As a writer of a straight historical crime book you can, however, learn something from pastiches. That is, that it is a considerable asset to have all the aspects of your novel reflecting the time you have chosen to set it in. Obviously your dialogue must be the speech of your period and the clothes you describe and the furnishings of your rooms must equally be in period. But there is something more. The whole action of your book should be in keeping with the action of books written at that particular time. So if you are producing a Victorian mystery, for instance, you would do well to think of a plot in terms more of melodrama than if you were writing a book set today.

So your research for this sort of book should be wider than the mere acquisition of facts about bustle skirts or togas or doublet and hose. You should do your best to sink yourself in the spirit of the age. Read the novels that were popular then, or the poetry or the plays.

And, of course, you should also be prepared to spend a good deal of time in looking out the everyday facts as well, those bustles and bonnets and antimacassars and plush tablecloths. But let me give you a particular tip here. It is those objects from distant days that are in some way in unexpected contrast to what we use today that are most effective in establishing in a reader's mind the ambience of those times. Bustles and antimacassars are fine, but most readers will add those from their own imaginations to any story set in Victorian times. What will give you that extra bite of interest is something like—and here I stop and open my indexed notebook of Victoriana (and I advise you to keep a similar book for your chosen period) and I find under 'B': boiled mutton on the sideboard for breakfast.

As to where you can find details of everyday life, there are of course, first the history books, particularly social history and such works as the multi-volume *History of Everyday Things in England* by Marjorie and D. H. B. Quennell (to be found in most public libraries of any size).

For the oddities I have spoken of go to the newspapers and novels of the period, where there are such things. I have found the advertisements in old newspapers a fine source of telling oddities. The novels of writers who are almost forgotten but who were popular in their day have also been particularly useful. The Victorians satisfied that universal appetite for soap operas, not with the theatre, but with the three-volume novel stuffed with the details of everyday life. You can often pick them up in second-hand bookshops.

On television, a most useful source open to the writer today but denied to those of earlier generations, are the programmes with historical settings. Most of these, as opposed to Hollywood films, go to immense trouble to get the details right, and by concentrating on the background rather than what's going on you can get a fine haul, especially with the aid of a video.

Once more, you want to aim with your research not just to acquire enough facts spread over your pages to give a feeling of the times, but to acquire so many that you have enough and to spare and can choose among your store for the one that does more than merely give a notion of the time you are writing about.

A detail should be used, where you can, for as many purposes simultaneously as possible. It can reflect the theme of your book as an object connected with whatever lies beneath what you are writing. It can reflect character by the attitude of one of the persons of your story towards it. It can be some object which will advance the action of your story. If you are very lucky it could perform all these functions at once.

Avoid the temptation of using too much of the material you have gathered. Details of life in the past should urge on your story, not show off your research. Oddly enough, the facts you have gathered and not used will not be wasted. They have entered your mind and there they add to the charge with which you are writing your book. They form, as it were, a heavy launching-pad from which your rocket will fly higher than if you had not known them.

Allied to this advice, I would counsel you to be very careful if you are using figures from real life in your story. One might think at first blush that a passing reference to a person that all your readers will have heard of would serve to authenticate your story. And so it might, provided it was only a passing mention and that it contributed properly to the pattern of the book.

But more than one such mention, or a too heavily insisted

on mention, especially when it is plain that it is not contributing to the whole, simply draws attention to the fact that you are producing fiction. There is an amusing passage from a skit by Max Beerbohm, the caricaturist and wit who flourished in the decadent 'nineties and the early years of this century, which neatly points out this danger. He is writing a parody of some historical drama and one of the stage directions goes:

> Enter Michael Angelo. Andrea del Sarto appears for a moment at a window. Pippa passes. Brothers of the Misericordia go by, singing a requiem for Francesca da Rimini. Enter Boccaccio, Benevenuto Cellini and many others, making remarks highly characteristic of themselves.

How not to do it!

Looking-back books

There are two more branches of the much-divided tree of crime fiction that we ought to glance at in our discussion of books set in the past. The first is the sub-genre that bases itself on events in the past that are perhaps not quite yet history. Where does the dividing line come between yesterday's news and the history books? There is no telling. But there are a number of crime novels that make use of the immediate past to excellent effect (Robert Barnard's *A Scandal in Belgravia* is one), and if the root causes of today's events are something that set your imagination bubbling then perhaps this is the sort of book you would be best to write. Of course, a large number of such stories on a less personal note come within the ambit of the espionage novel and as such without the ambit of this book. But they can be pure crime fiction and fine crime fiction too.

Perhaps it is your childhood days that haunt your imagination and you would like to set a book some twenty, thirty or forty years back. This is hardly history but it is the past, and for those of us who are filled with wonder at those days, the past can give a powerful charge to one's writing. All that is needed is plenty of recall, supplemented perhaps by some memory-tickling research. Here again the newspapers of the day, when you can get hold of them, are the best source. The British Library newspaper library at Colindale Avenue, London NW9, is the place to apply for a reader's ticket if you are within reach. Otherwise your local paper should have files.

Of course, you also need a crime to write your crime fiction about, a story thread for your feelings of nostalgia. The more characteristic of its time your crime is the better your book will be. So take time to choose. Think what sort of murders were most in the public eye at the period you want to write about, because there are fashions in murder. George Orwell has a fascinating essay on this subject called *The Decline of the English Murder*, the title also of the paperback collection of essays in which it appears. Read it and see what I mean. Once, he says, respectability was what lay behind the murders that the public wanted to read about (remember Edgar Wallace saying vanity was the basic murder motive), but then the fashion changed.

What was it at the period in the recent past that fascinates you? Find it, and you may have a crime to write about that will let you bring to vivid life the social customs and curiosities of a day before yesterday.

Real crime into fiction

Real crimes used as the subject (not the theme) for books of fiction provide yet another branch on the great tree that we should look at. You may feel that an idea of this sort is what will give you the most charge to get through the sixty, seventy or eighty thousand words that lie between you and a finished manuscript, let alone the weeks of researching that may be necessary and the dense hours of hard thinking.

Generally the subject is some particularly notorious crime in the past. (Don't of course, write about any fairly recent case in which the accused was found Not Guilty, however attractive your theories about it.) There have been dozens, perhaps hundreds of novels, however, written about the great mysteries of crime from the Constance Kent case of the 1860s to the Wallace trial (The Was-there-a-Mr-Qualtrough case) of 1931 to the mystery of who killed the Princes in the Tower, a subject to choose only if you think you can beat the redoubtable Josephine Tey's classic *The Daughter of Time*. But, note, that is more a crime novel about twisted truth.

There is still room for others. The only difficulty, but it is a considerable one, is that the writer whatever theories he or she may develop is bound by a special clause in the invisible contract with the reader to stick absolutely to any known facts. One has to make sure of finding these out first. But the real mysteries are all well documented, and you will have no need to hunt down obscure sources.

Once sure of your facts, exercise your ingenuity. Hit, if you can, on some explanation of one of these mysteries that has not been put forward before, and go ahead. You will be at liberty to invent any dialogue, any actions not contradicted by the known facts and to put what interpretation you like on your characters' actions. And you have the framework of your story ready made for you, a great help to the beginner.

The crime short story

One last, last branch of crime fiction, the short story. And almost I am tempted to make my advice about writing it just one word—Don't.

Don't because there is at present, and has been for a good many years past, almost nowhere to publish the stories you may write.

Don't, too, because it's a very difficult thing to do, attractive though it looks when, instead of producing anything of between sixty and eighty thousand words, all you have got to do is to produce, say, as few as one thousand. But constructing a plot for a crime short story can on occasion be as demanding as constructing a plot for a whole crime novel. And, to descend to crude practicalities, you are going to get very much less money for what you have done, though it is only fair to add that if you are lucky and clever enough to create a story that catches the editors' fancies then it can be anthologised time and again and in the end bring in perhaps as much as a full-length book that has failed to get wide paperback sales.

Yet the fundamental fact remains that there is nowadays much, much less demand than there once was for the crime short story. Blame television, of course. And, for once, with some justice. The demand for a little something to take the mind off the day's troubles is now much more fulfilled by a soap opera or a half-hour crime story on the telly. The wealth of fiction available from that source has even scared evening newspaper editors off using short stories, let alone crime short stories, as they once did almost every day.

The crime short story was not always so little wanted. The

whole great crime story wave that began in the last years of the nineteenth century and rose to its towering peak in the 1920s and 1930s began with the short story. It began in fact with what are perhaps still the best crime short stories to be found; the tales of Sherlock Holmes. These, as they appeared one by one in the pages of the *Strand Magazine*, attracted enormous popularity. Their success in gripping the public mind can be compared today only to the most avidly watched television programmes. Perhaps the stories were even more popular, for when Conan Doyle decided in 1894 to kill off his hero, so that he could write serious books, historical novels, there was such an outcry that bands of young men wearing black armbands marched on the *Strand Magazine* office.

Of course, Doyle's success brought imitators by the score, all writing then in the short story form. There were the creators of supermen roughly in the Holmes mould and generally attempting to excel him, like the American Jacques Futrelle with his hero Professor Augustus S. F. X. Van Dusen, the Thinking Machine, or, in a slightly different mould, G. K. Chesterton with his spiritual, though humble, superman, Father Brown, a genuine Great Detective.

On the other hand, there were the numerous authors who attempted to trump Conan Doyle's ace by having extremely unsupermen heroes. One of the first of these, treading closely on the Holmes' heels, was Arthur Morrison, author of two novels still current, *A Child of the Jago* and *The Hole in the Wall*, who appears to have built his Martin Hewitt, private investigator, almost as an exact opposite of Holmes. His cases were apt to be commonplace affairs, or at least to begin as such, as opposed to the affairs of state that occupied Holmes in his latter years, and where Holmes was tall and hawk-faced Hewitt was stoutish, of average height and had a round, smiling face.

Authors in both traditions happily wrote away in the footsteps of the great Sherlock for a good many years after his second, slightly less flamboyant departure from the scene. There were, too, plenty of places for their stories to be published.

But, stealthily, all the while the detective story at novel length was gaining in popularity. This was, perhaps, because there was an increasing number of women readers with leisure to spend a whole afternoon buried in a book from the lending library, institutions which flourished mightily in the years between 1918 and 1945 and even somewhat later. But then there came the great god Telly, and for the short story all was darkness.

Or nearly all. Because crime short stories have continued to be written and some of the very best of them have appeared in the Television Age. They present a challenge to the writer. So, despite poor rewards, even the ultimate poor reward of death in the ever-shut drawer, they get written.

Yet their nature has, on the whole, changed. Detective short stories are still produced, but they have been thrust firmly into second place, both in the minds of writers and readers, by the crime short story. This, to use a definition of the American, Stanley Ellin, one of the writers to have given us short stories to equal any that have been written since crime and the short story met (read his *The Speciality of the House*) is any story so long as it deals with 'that streak of wickedness in human nature'. It is the equivalent of the crime novel we have already analysed.

So much for the subject. But what about the way that the subject, that streak of wickedness, is handled? Let's hear from Stan Ellin again. He is talking this time of the short stories of Guy de Maupassant, only a few of which can perhaps be seized on as crime short stories before their time. Ellin says that he could tell even as a sixteen-year-old that 'here was a writer who reduced stories to their absolute essence' and, he adds, the ending of each de Maupassant story is, when you think about it, 'as inevitable as doom'.

Two tough precepts to follow. But they should be aimed at if you are writing in short story form the equivalent of the crime novel. Happily, there are what the ski people call 'nursery slopes'. There is a type of short story in crime fiction which does not make the highest demands on its writers, though it is not as easy as the gentlest of ski runs.

This is what I have called, in reviewing, the switch-over story. It is perhaps hardly more than an anecdote, generally quite short in length, in which towards the end the reader, who has been gently led along one seemingly well-defined path, is suddenly switched into seeing the situation in quite a different light.

Let me give you an example. It is a story by Ruth Rendell, a writer with prizes under her belt in the art of the crime short story. Called *Born Victim* it begins 'I murdered Brenda Goring for what I suppose is the most unusual of motives. She came between me and my wife'.

The narrator then goes on to tell of this divorcee, Brenda Goring, who arrives in their village and who latches on to his quiet mouse of a wife, whom he dearly loves, fills her ears with tales of the fast life she has always led and still leads in visits to London and, worse, is always to be found in his home when he gets back exhausted from the office. But amusingly, he soon discovers that Brenda is in fact frigid and that her accounts of London lovers are the fantasies of a compulsive liar. However, he feels he cannot disillusion his tender plant of a wife, and so is saddled with Brenda for ever. He decides to kill her, and to this end pretends to be particularly friendly with her. His opportunity comes when a lone housewife is murdered by a psychopath and shortly after he himself catches 'flu and reckons he can trick the doctor into giving him an alibi that he is too ill to get out of bed. So off he goes and murders Brenda. Only to find, first, that genuinely ill as he was, he had missed the local paper saying the psychopath had been caught, and that the compulsive liar Brenda had been telling everyone he was her lover, a rumour that had got back to his wife whose mac he had by mistake worn during the murder and had been unable to destroy.

Now comes the end. The wife, we learn, is the one who is about to be tried for the crime, and nothing the narrator has been able to say has convinced the police he himself is the guilty man.

See how it's done? The first sentence setting up the idea in the reader's mind that not only has the narrator committed a murder but that something has gone wrong and he has, despite all precautions, been found out. Then the subtly laid twist. The switch-over.

Of course, the whole odd train of events is most unlikely to have happened in real life. But Ruth Rendell, here, is not trying to describe anything that might truly have happened. She is playing a game with us, and playing it delightfully well.

A similar switch-over type of story can be written by doing what I have counselled writers of full-length detective stories not to do: by slipping in a tiny clue in the hope that readers will miss it. In this anecdotal kind of story the device is, on the whole, pleasing to the reader, even after being caught out by it, and so it is permissible. It might take the form of one small spelling mistake or an Americanism coming from someone stated as not being American or a supposedly deaf person repeating a quietly spoken remark; anything on those lines.

Yet beware. You are under an obligation not to use any little piece of knowledge which it is too much to expect your readers to know. And who are your readers? And how much should they know? Unanswerable questions, really. It is a matter of judgement. Even the great ones can falter here. There is a story of Dorothy L. Sayers that depends on the reader noting that a French speaker uses in one careless word the wrong gender and thus, supposedly, gives himself away as a man masquerading as a woman. To my mind, this is asking too much.

A slightly more complex form of the crime short story, and one which can pay considerable dividends in reader enjoyment, is what one might call the plain puzzle story with a solution coming from cunning detective work, both by the sleuth and the reader. This is in miniature the classic blueprint detective story, and it can give more pleasure by virtue of its clues coming closer to the final revelation than sometimes the full-length affair does. The gasp of delight is all the stronger for the trick played being nearer to hand.

Perhaps the best way to write this kind of story (or even the equivalent of the detective novel at short story length) is to do as I did with the first crime short story I ever wrote. I had decided to enter for a competition for British crime writers, run a good many years ago by *Ellery Queen's Mystery Magazine*. But I found I had little idea how to set about producing a crime short story. In the end I simply did what I had done in writing at full length but I compressed the whole into the 5000-word stipulated maximum length. It won second prize.

One possible reason for its comparative success, and one which I stumbled on in all innocence at that time, was that its subject and setting were limited. It seems that limited settings or subjects are particularly suited to the crime short story. They can be some branch of sport, for instance, (sport is hard to use in a full-length book) or the atmosphere of some small closed society. My story was of a murder taking place in a boys' preparatory boarding school ('looking-back book' in miniature, in fact) with the victim being a pet bird. But otherwise it had all the ingredients of the detective novel, down to a theme, the passion for justice.

This leads us back to considering not the detective short story but the crime short story, the equivalent of the crime novel we have looked at, one of those stories which has in it no more than, in Stan Ellin's words, 'that streak of something wicked'.

Where the detective short story had as its object the displaying of an act of detection, the crime short story or suspense short story has as its object to put a person or persons into danger and give a revelation to one or more people, be they the perpetrator of a crime, its victim or simply a witness. Where in the detective short story ingenuity was, in principle, the only quality called for, in the crime short story ingenuity has to be at the service of imagination. I say 'in principle' because, life being what it is, there are many occasions when it is impossible to say whether a story is a pure detection affair or one partaking of more of the crime element.

Among these borderline cases will come the short-story version of the inverted detective story we have already looked at, the story where the murderer is known to the reader from the outset and the pleasure lies in seeing how, inadvertently, he betrays himself, or she herself. Again, because of the shorter distance between premise and fulfilment, the inverted story at short length can be more pleasure-giving than in the more difficult book-length form. But otherwise all the rules for writing it apply, in miniature.

The same goes, too, for locked-room stories. At a length of between 2000 and 5000 words these are highly satisfying: at 60 000 words they can become tediously frivolous. Much the same comment can be applied to comic crime. Although in the hands of a master like Donald E. Westlake the full-length comic crime story can dazzle for 70 000 words or more, at the hands of a less expert practitioner the very repetition of good or goodish jokes can become fatiguing to the reader. Not so at the short story length, where humour can be used more gainfully to put over the perhaps dull facts needed to lay out a situation leading to an ingenious switch-over ending.

So what guidance can I give for the actual writing of the crime short story? First, the first thing, the very beginning words. Think back to the ones I quoted of Ruth Rendell's story *Born Victim*, 'I murdered Brenda Goring for what I suppose is the most unusual of motives. She came between me and my wife.' It would be a tough-minded individual who could lay down that story after reading those two short sentences.

So, go to a considerable amount of trouble to, first, find the point where your story has to begin, where the first absolutely necessary fact has to be put before the reader, then work equally hard to find a form of words to state it that will catch your reader as firmly as Ruth Rendell catches hers.

Next, bear in mind the lesson Stan Ellin learnt as a teenager from Guy de Maupassant and reduce what you have to tell to its absolute essence. Much of the pleasure of the short story lies in its very shortness. And, finally, of course, get your surprise, or whatever other ending you have, perhaps a sad down-plunging note, as near to the actual end as you can.

But what among all the streaks of wickedness in human nature are you going to write about? My own experience, on the rare occasions when I have actually been asked to produce a short story with my mind totally blank, is that one can tune oneself like the strings of a wind-harp by admitting to one's mind the desire to write a story and that in that state of receptivity even the oddest, most trivial circumstances will produce a basic idea. I remember once feeling this when, walking along a suburban road in the half-light, I nearly stumbled over a bump in the ground. And a story came into my head.

Daphne Du Maurier in her *The Rebecca Notebook* said she would, when in France, just sit in a cafe and let the conversation or the attitudes of the people at nearby tables gradually impinge. If this does not work (and I don't think you actually have to go to France), you might try the recipe of the American crime short story writer, Robert Twohy, who writes out a first sentence and then sees if anything comes from it, and so on. I gather there are times when the mission aborts, but on the other hand he has sold many and many a story to *Ellery Queen's Mystery Magazine*.

The crime short story is perhaps the most difficult branch of crime fiction to write, except in the mere matter of the number of times it is necessary to put finger to word-processor key. Yet it is there. It holds out a challenge. Few crime writers can resist it for ever. If at the beginning of a career in crime writing you feel you would like to try this most awkward of short climbs, good luck to you.

5
How to Begin, Go On and Finish

The detective story is a story. The crime novel is a novel. Crime fiction is fiction. So what you are doing in writing crime fiction is writing fiction like any other fiction, except that you will be working in one of the modes we have analysed. You will be keeping within the parameters we have laid down, but within them doing what all other novelists do, creating worlds that do not exist but giving them the feeling, to a greater or lesser extent, of really existing.

So what I have to say in this chapter will apply by and large to writing any form of fiction.

And the first possible problem that confronts us is: how do you begin to do this at all? It is common for any author who has produced more than one or two books to hear people casually met saying, 'But I wouldn't have any idea how to begin'. Though I myself never had any difficulty over this (largely because it never occurred to my innocent young self that the difficulty existed), I can well understand how somebody can want to write, even know that what they would like to produce is a work of crime fiction, but yet baulk at actually beginning.

My advice to the people I meet at parties and elsewhere who say 'I wouldn't know where to start' takes the form of offering them first a harp and then some porridge.

The harp—it is actually a wind-harp, a set of taut strings which currents of air cause to emit musical notes—we have already met. I use it as an analogy for the state of simply but strongly wishing to produce any particular sort of fiction. Only want strongly enough to do this, I believe, and you will tune your mind, or perhaps your subconscious, to a state where almost anything you see, do or hear will trigger off an idea for a story or a book. Often a quiet look at an apparently ridiculous idea will show that it is not as way-out as it seems. Indeed, a degree of absurdity in an idea is probably a good

thing. It means that the book or story that eventually comes
from it will have that certain differentness that marks out the
better books from the average, and often the average ones fail
to move from the chrysalis of a typescript to the butterfly of
an actual published book.

But porridge? Well, it occurred to me once that producing
a book is not unlike producing a bowl of porridge. For some
reason, or almost none, you find yourself with a dry idea that
might make a book, a handful of porridge oats. You drop this
idea into the water-pot of your subconscious, and then you
heat it with that fire of the imagination I have perhaps
referred to too often in these pages, and you stir it with the
wooden spoon of reason, of simple rational thought applied
as it were from the outside.

As you bring these two opposed forces to your small handful of oats they begin to swell. You stir on and you keep that
heat of the imagination playing and gradually the porridge
thickens and thickens, flake attaches itself to flake, idea to
idea, till eventually you have, not some water and a scatter-
ing of dry oats, but a single coagulated and possibly even
delicious mass. Serve, with the sugar of publisher's publicity
(a modest sprinkling) and the milk of an attractive dust-
jacket.

What will that handful of dry oats consist of, however?
I would be giving you less help than I ought if I left it at that.
But the answer is that the idea which triggers off a book can
be very different from writer to writer. With Dick Francis, he
once said to me, it is something tangible such as happening
to find out a little about the business of air taxi-ing or at a
dinner party meeting someone who ran a kidnapping insur-
ance business. With myself, on the other hand, it is, as I have
already said, something as nebulous as wondering how
perfect we ought to be in the business of daily life or happening to read a tiny news item about kidnappers in Japan
taking, not the son of the rich man, but his chauffeur's son
and wondering briefly what the rich man must have felt; a
moment of reflection which became, with the porridge oats
stirred and stirred, a book called *Inspector Ghote Trusts the
Heart*.

But whether, as with myself, it is generally the theme of the
book that comes as the idea for it, or whether as with Dick
Francis it is the subject, the background, that comes first, it is
always a good thing to work back to that theme. Ask yourself,

as I did when for a change the notion of writing a detective novel with the background of croquet came to me, what is it about that subject that has made me so interested in it? In my case it turned out to be, by contrast with the seeming placidity of a game of croquet, violence. I realised that violence, whether we can avoid it altogether or whether in fact it is inescapable and even necessary, was what bugged me fundamentally. From that, with the gas ring under the porridge turned up to full and the wooden spoon stirring and stirring, came a book with various and varied violent people in it called, from a croquet term, *A Rush on the Ultimate*.

Note that 'with various and varied violent people'. Once you have stirred the porridge that first time or two and made sure what your theme is and what is your subject, one layer higher up, you will begin to want to know who is going to act out the vague story you have in mind. Because people are fiction. With the rare exception of stories about animals (and these in any case are usually humans in disguise) people are the very stuff of these imitations of the real world that we have set out to create. Of course, life being messy you will no doubt simultaneously be toying with thoughts of your plot as well as your people, but let us order the mess a little (it's what novelists do, after all) and consider the people, the characters, first.

And, as I have said, you will want to make these, as far as you can, people reflecting whatever theme you are putting as the foundation for your book. But this is to see them in a fairly dry-as-dust manner, almost like the characters in Bunyan; Mr Steadfast, Mr Worldly Wiseman etc. To add something more lifelike, more complex, to stick two of your porridge flakes together, you can hardly do better than to look round at your acquaintances and see which seem to link up with your basic, Bunyanish ideas. On the whole, don't look at your family or close friends. You know too much about them. They will bring along, with whatever aspect of their character you have fixed on, a whole heap of other qualities which will only clog up the picture you want to paint.

Indeed, you may need people even less well known to you than acquaintances. Tune your wind-harp again and keep your ears and eyes open, as the young Agatha Christie did when she was intent on producing her first detective story, *The Mysterious Affair at Styles*. In her autobiography she tells how, having the vaguest of plots in mind, she was in a tram in Torquay when she saw 'a man with a black beard sitting next to an elderly lady who was chattering like a magpie'. And she had been wanting a mysterious-looking figure as her murderer. (Read the book, and see what good use she eventually made of that beard.) Sitting nearby, she adds, was 'a large, hearty woman, talking loudly about spring bulbs'. That was all young Agatha needed. She immediately 'knew' the hearty woman's name, Evelyn. A stir with the spoon and she saw that Evelyn could be a poor relation, a lady gardener or a companion. And one of the suspects, of course.

She knew the name. Naming your people is an important part of thickening them up. Once you decide on a name, and it is best to let the intuitive side of the brain do the deciding, as Agatha Christie did, the character will take on extra life in your imagination.

So try to avoid slapping on a label like 'John Smith'. Find, or let your subconscious find, a name that subtly says something about the person. Don't be as blatant as Bunyan and fix on Mr Worldly Wiseman (Bunyan was a genius) but be, if you can, as lucky as Conan Doyle and produce Professor Moriarty (hint of death there, I think, la mort, and a certain grim heaviness) or Dr Grimesby Roylott, the villain in the Speckled Band affair, (Grime, of course, with its hint of ineradicable dirt, plus Roy, the touch of the king that indicated the old family he came from and power, too) or Charles Augustus Milverton, 'the worst man in London', the blackmailer. (The aura of inflated respectability in the forenames and the slightest hint of the snake that Milverton is later compared to in that long thin vowel of the first syllable of the family name, together with the length of the whole.)

At the same time as finding a name for a character it is a good idea (well, it's what I do myself) to attach to them one typical trait. You can even, when you first come to describe this person, exaggerate this trait so that at each later appearance you have only to mention the trait or refer to it in the most oblique manner for the character to spring fully back to life in your reader's mind: a tip I got from reading some academic tome about the great Joseph Conrad.

Let me follow that with a hint I once got from reading something about the great film-maker, Renoir. He said that in building up a character he liked to do what he did with the camera, to isolate the main look of the person in black and white and then to put in as much as he dared of grey; grey taking away from that first black and white image. If you do this, put in as much as you dare of the opposite of whatever first bold picture you had of a person while still keeping the original present, then you will be both thickening that character and making him or her more lifelike. Aren't we all, after all, a mass of contradictions?

This is the wooden spoon at work stirring, the giving of hard, rational thought to what it is you are doing. But at the same time your subconscious, if you are intent enough on the book you are gradually bringing into life, will be working away for you too. The water in the pot will be bubbling, swelling the porridge flakes. It will give you sudden flashes of insight into your characters, sudden unexpected twists to your plot, sudden new scenes for your story.

Seize its offerings. When I am in the early stages of a book I carry everywhere a very small notepad. And I do not hesitate, odd looks or no odd looks, to stop just where I am when up into my outer mind there floats a thought to jot it down.

Gregory Macdonald, the American crime writer, recommends the cultivation not of memory but of forgettory with regard to ideas, and his point is a good one. Perhaps only the ideas that will not be forgotten, try as you may, are the ones sturdy enough to make a good book. But his advice should not apply to this stage of the proceedings. You have had your initial idea. You have failed to forget it. So now you should be working on it, both with the spoon and burning heat, and you should make sure you don't lose any of the products.

Your little notepad (if you take my advice) should not be confused with your notebook. I think almost all writers have a notebook for each novel they write. My own take more or less this form:

- I allow a page or perhaps a double page to each character;

- I allow a page for each chapter (no logical need to have chapters, but readers like them and they are a useful handrail as you plunge through the stormy seas of telling your story);

- at the end of the notebook I make out a list of the scenes I have split the story up into, with the page of the first draft on which each begins (very useful when adding necessary bits in revision);

- on the inside cover I make a list of the names I intend to use (it helps me not to have a Lovell and a Lowry in the same book);

● somewhere in the first few pages I write out in large letters what the theme is, and my answers to Professor Donald Davie's questions about its relation to the central action, plus perhaps a stern admonition or two like 'Remember the Reader';

● then, in however many pages are necessary, first I write out the basic plot, then usually I write it out again when I have arrived at a more detailed version;

● and next I use however many pages are necessary to write out the events of the story in brief, what I have called (since it helps me to think lineally) the storyline;

● and wherever there is room left over I conduct arguments with myself when I come to some knotty point I can't see how to get round. Two columns, Pro and Con, often sort me out, or even simply writing out a question like 'Why does Harriet go into the empty house now?' Often before I've finished putting down the words Old Subconscious squirts me up the answer: 'She was afraid of the frogs on the path in front of her'. Ridiculous, but lifelike.

Parallel with mulling over the people of your story (and that, incidentally, is something you can do whenever there's a quiet moment all through the day) you will have been puzzling over your plot. But the word 'plot' is apt to be used loosely, and for our purposes what it is should be absolutely clear.

Let me borrow some often quoted words from the novelist, E. M. Forster, in a little book called *Aspects of the Novel*, one you would almost certainly benefit from although it was written as long ago as 1927 (libraries often have reprints). 'Let us define plot,' he says. 'We have defined story as a narrative of events, the emphasis falling on causality. "The king died and then the queen died" is a story. "The king died, and then the queen died of grief" is a plot.' He goes on to give another example of plot 'The queen died, no one knew why, until it was discovered that it was through grief at the death of the king.' That, he said, is a plot with a mystery in it, a form capable of high development. Nota bene.

So what you will have to do, to a greater or lesser extent depending on the type of crime fiction you are at work on, is to plan what will happen, with the emphasis on what has caused each successive event. But besides planning you would do well at this stage to begin planting.

What is planting? Planting is the slipping in as mere hints at an early stage things that will later bulk large. It is somewhat different from inserting the clues of the classical detective story, or such of its successors, where clues are wanted. What a planted item foreshadows does not need to be anything as concrete as the item a clue foreshadows. It can be a tiny hint about an aspect of a person's character that is going to become more important, as for instance a casual 'he said, helping himself to more pudding' when the character's greediness is going to play a considerable part in later events.

But not only is planting important for building up such key parts of a book, it is also extremely useful as a means of establishing credibility. Mention something indirectly at an early stage, and when later you need to have the reader believe in that item the very fact of it having, so to speak, already happened will make it somehow more solid in the reader's mind. You can, of course, also work backwards with this, seizing on some tiny thing your subconscious has presciently provided and making more of it at a later stage of your book.

So, you have made notes about your characters, writing down what particular traits you feel will most distinguish them, and—a help towards getting them one degree thicker— their ages and perhaps some other broad details about them which you will not necessarily ever mention in the final pages, lifting them from the fuller essays you may have written about them as I suggested earlier. You have, too, written out your plot perhaps both in its basic form in, say, half a page and in something approaching its final form. You have looked at this plot and from it seen what your storyline must be and you have written that down. You have allocated chunks of the storyline to each of your proposed chapters, probably between twenty and thirty of them. And now you're ready to go.

Fearful moment. I always liken it to standing on a high diving-board above a very small swimming pool, full of icy water. But dive you must.

And if you can you should dive with a neat splash. Or, put it another way, you need a good opening line, if only because in bookshops or libraries potential readers will flick open your book and glance at the first few words. So tell a riddle. By which I don't mean produce a specific conundrum, but find a first line that asks a question, even the tiniest of questions. Your reader will hardly be able not to want to know the answer, and so will read—it's a beginning—your second sentence.

Let me give an example from one of my own books: 'Inspector Ghote stood too rigidly at attention . . .' A reader at once asks, I hope, why is this man, whoever he is, standing 'too rigidly'? The answer comes soon enough. Ghote is in front of his boss getting orders and he is over-anxious. But by the time that is clear there will be some other tiny riddle the reader will want to know the answer to.

Not only is Sentence One important, but Page One is, too. I have in reviewing read many a Page One into which the writer has tried to put too much. Yes, at the beginning of a book there are lots of things you have got to establish. But as you write that first page—and you will probably have to rewrite and rewrite it—think of the reader, think how much he or she is likely to be able properly to absorb; ask yourself of every fact you put down, 'Do I absolutely need this now?' Certainly don't have more than two people in your first page mentioned by name, one of whom should be in most circumstances your hero or heroine. And, since dialogue makes for unstoppable reading, try to get at least the start of a conversation in the first 300 words you write.

At a conference for crime writers recently I heard the editor at one crime publisher say she always judges a typescript on just the first three pages. Tough talk. But from my own experience as a reviewer I can confirm it largely. I remember very few books which belied what the writer had put on paper in those few beginning pages.

And, of course, next only in importance for reader-grabbing to Page One is Chapter One. If you can get your reader to the end of Chapter One and wanting more, you have in all probability hooked your fish right to the end of the book. So you must get into this first chapter a conflict. It should be a reasonably strong conflict and one with a considerable degree of human interest, though by no means necessarily does it have to take a physical form. A ding-dong argument does very well. And remember, this conflict has got to be topped by a yet better one and that one by one yet better. So take a tip from my actress wife and pace yourself. Don't give your first big scene everything you've got or you will be left with nowhere to go for your last big scene.

And end this first chapter, as with variations you should end each chapter, with what I in my notes to myself have called a 'forward-pointer', something—it need be only the quickest of hints—that tells the reader there is something interesting ahead. This is another example of the riddle I spoke of as being necessary for your opening words. Or, as the American novelist John Updike said in an interview for the literary magazine *Paris Review* (scores of the magazine's interviews are collected in four Penguin volumes and are well worth mulling over), 'I try instantly to set in motion a certain forward tilt of suspense or curiosity'.

Going on

I have referred, in counselling you to have a notebook for your book, to a list of 'scenes' and in citing my wife's experience as an actress I again spoke of 'scenes', and I think to attain vividness in entertainment fiction the seeing of your book in terms of scenes, as in a theatre, is decidedly valuable. Of course, there will in all probability be passages where, to forward your story, you will have to rely on pure narration. But make these, if you take my advice, as few as possible. Ask yourself of any point you have to make whether it cannot be put over as drama. And end each such scene, as I have advised you to end each chapter, with a forward-pointer. I sometimes list these in advance in my schedule of 'scenes'.

Drama, Alfred Hitchcock once said, 'is like real life with the dull bits cut out'. And Hercule Poirot chimes in 'Murder is drama. The desire for drama is very strong in the human race.'

But, alas, it is not quite as easy as that. Drama is fine. But it will fail in its effect if you fill your pages with scenes of high drama bang one up against another. Any such scene is the more effective for being preceded by a period of tranquility.

Sometimes at the start of one of these quieter patches you can hint that fireworks are ahead, and this can be extremely effective. Having given the reader that incentive you can pack in a lot of the duller facts you may need to put over as part of your plot or you can put in some of the facts of any background you are using. I have myself more than once told readers that at the end of a journey through the jam-packed streets of Bombay Inspector Ghote is likely to find himself in a scene of drama, and then I have described that journey, the details of Bombay life as seen through a car window. It is infuriating to readers. But it is the sort of infuriatingness that they find enjoyable.

Another use to be made of the pause before the storm is to

hark back after a preceding storm and fill in details that would have clogged up your action scene which, remember, Graham Greene says should consist of little more than subject, verb, object. In such pauses, too, in the early stages of a book you can work in those facts you have sternly made yourself cut out of that opening page.

It is, broadly speaking, all a matter of pace, and I will not pretend that acquiring the right sense of pace is an easy matter. You could, of course, over long years become a champion jockey like Dick Francis, and then the art you acquired over the jumps would mysteriously serve you over the pages. Perhaps a critical, careful study of the Francis books will help you to ride, as it were, on his shoulders.

Pace, I say to myself somewhere in my writer's notebook, is like driving. 'Just as with a car, there is a right speed for every stretch of road, so with a book it is wrong to go too fast over major acts, wrong to linger too long on the trivial.' Good advice, if depressingly lacking in particularity,

Advice of a rather more practical nature I once got from the late Margery Allingham, who got it in her turn, I believe, from some now forgotten writer of a previous generation. It simply goes like this: get in a surprise every ten pages and a shock every twenty. Crude—and, of course, you don't need to carry it out to the letter. Yet I have found that it is no bad thing, in this entertainment fiction we are writing, to look over the storyline for a book and ask myself whether I am providing surprises and shocks at about those intervals, depending needless to say to some extent on the type of book. A thriller would need its shocks this often or even more frequently; a crime novel would need many fewer but still a good ration of surprises.

A shock we can define as the sudden revelation of something totally unexpected (though your reader afterwards should say, because of what you have planted, 'Why, yes, of course that was bound to happen'). A surprise we might define as the sudden contrivance of an intriguing situation, often of quite minor proportions. It can also be called a 'twist'.

Be careful, however, in working towards your coming shock or surprise of the way you use that trick of telling the reader something exciting is coming and then making them wait. Do not give the game away in advance. When you yourself know what is going to happen it is extraordinarily easy to write your 'advance warning' in such a way that you steal your own thunder. A reviewer once said about one of my straight novels, rather cruelly I think, that each time a plan for some future action was laid out you knew it was going to fail, but when no plan was described you could be sure the following action would be a success. It is all right to say 'Next day was to see a turning point in John's life' and then to make your reader wait; it is not all right to say 'Next day was to bring all John's hopes to an end'.

As to the nature of the twists you might use, I have loosely stuck in my notebook a yellowing cutting of an interview with the situation comedy writer, Denis Norden. In it he says 'You get a complicated situation, and "second guess" people as to the next twist. It's like a conjuring trick. The audience knows the rabbit is going to disappear—you know that, or there's no point in it being there. It's the misdirection that matters, so that what does happen is not what everyone thinks is going to happen.' John Braine in his book *Writing A Novel* put it in much the same way in an analogy which has always struck me as being very vivid. Telling a story, he said, is like going along bouncing a ball. A watcher knows it is going to come up to your hand again, but you make it do so from a direction the watcher doesn't expect.

It is not only in action scenes that this storytelling device can be used. It works just as well for those possibly boring scenes that have to appear in most crime fiction, the interviews. Your reader will know that the person being interviewed or interrogated by your hero is going to come up with a certain sort of answer, maybe a confession, maybe a lie, maybe a blank refusal to co-operate, according to the situation you have led up to. The trick is to make that confession or lie or refusal come not quite in the way it looks as if it is going to. The readers then get the surprise that sends them rapidly on for the next twenty pages.

Interviews then need not be dull, especially as there is a whole range of different approaches to getting information out of a reluctant witness and you can show any or all of them in action. Your hero, or heroine, can create in the witness's mind sympathy, or anxiety. They can use silence or exhaustion or bluff or cajolery or insinuation or threat.

Here is something I typed laboriously out for my notebook years ago, in the pre-copyshop era, from a novel, *The Flypaper War*, by an author called Richard Starnes, who had worked for the noted Scripps-Howard newspaper chain in America.

He describes his hero, also a newspaper man, as an interviewer. He could, he says, assume a naivety which induced carelessness in concealing information or he could bluntly declare he knew more than he did and so trick an interviewee. He could grope for words and let the interviewee supply them. He could be stupid, wise, friendly, angry, cynical, trusting, indifferent or deeply concerned as the occasion demanded. Plenty of scope there in writing an interview scene!

One other type of passage you may need to use which might be thought likely to hold up the onward progress of your story is explanations. Despite what R. Austin Freeman believed about the final explanation in a detective story being the most interesting part, most readers are apt to get bored as you account for the ingenious things you have done earlier at as much length as may be necessary (and this, of course, applies more or less to other types of crime fiction than the classical detective story). So how can you get round the difficulty?

One thing to do, it should go without saying, is to look at what you have written and fine it down to the utmost. Another is to mingle your explanation with action. A little crude, this. How often have you read that climactic scene where the hero, dodging bullets, hears the villain explain his master-plan? Crude, yes. But undeniably useful. Yet another way is to sprinkle the passage of explanation with jokes or characteristically comic behaviour from one of your people. A fourth, and excellent way is to have a character make the explanations while simply doing something—it may be as mundane as packing a suitcase—in a tremendous hurry. The reader gets infected by the air of haste and whizzes through the long explanation.

So far I have been dealing with storytelling concerned with short periods of time, as most crime fiction requires. But there may be occasions in a book where a good many months or years have to pass, and it is worth looking at ways of making this happen in a convincing manner.

One way of not doing it (which is yet quite frequently done) is to label chapters with dates. This might seem the simplest way of telling the reader that time has passed. But, curiously, because such labels fall outside the text readers are apt, not exactly to miss them, but to discount them. It is a tribute, if you like, to the power of fiction. While the reader is in your grasp he believes only in the world you are telling him about in your continuing story.

This, to digress a little, is a good reason for avoiding the use of what has been called 'the authorial voice', that is, speaking to your readers in your own voice. It can be done, and can be a most effective device—in the hands of a master. Trollope frequently uses the device, and paradoxically, by stepping outside his story and commenting on perhaps even his method of telling it he somehow makes you believe all the more firmly that these people, who he has said are his fictional creations, are nevertheless real. I think it is because he gets his readers so very firmly into his grasp. But in the hands of lesser writers 'author speaking' just draws attention to the artificiality of what you are doing.

So, to revert, how are you to indicate the passing of time? Well, the good old traditional ways are still perfectly valid. 'Now it was winter and the trees that six months ago . . .' or ' "I am very much disliking this July weather," said Inspector Ghote.' But the main way of conveying that time has passed is to convince yourself absolutely that it has. Then you will not make tiny errors, unnoticed directly by almost all your readers, but nevertheless secretly doing the damage. And, totally convinced, you will put in, unconsciously, the tiny things that subtly show the situation is not as it was, say, six months earlier.

Finally, remember that the story is, particularly in entertainment fiction, the writer's most potent weapon. Telling a story may get in the way of all sorts of things that you would rather be sliding into your readers' heads. But it is something that has to be given first consideration. We all of us live in the successive passing of moments, and to see life in any other way is asking us to do a very difficult thing. So the novelist who wants to make things as easy as possible for the reader must be prepared to say what he has to in the form of a story, of the succession of events.

So ask yourself at each turn in your book what it is that the reader will want to know next. Give the reader that, and not something that perhaps you want the reader to learn. But remember John Braine's bouncing ball, and give that next thing to your readers in a way that will slightly surprise them.

And be interested yourself in your story. One might think that this was obvious. But I have reviewed books where it has abruptly become clear to me that the writer was not really interested in his story. His interest might have been in the particular background or setting he was writing of, or in one of the characters, and a story had been perfunctorily chosen and was being slackly laid out. Don't make that mistake. Worry around until you hit on a story that passionately interests you and then in your hands you have a mighty weapon.

Finishing

Sooner or later, after 60 000 or 80 000 words, you will have to lay down the weapon of story, and it is worth considering a little the way to do that. I speak from sharp experience. I think that out of all the novels I have written, and since 1959 there have been quite a few, there can have been only two or at the most three when my wife, reading the messy typescript of the first draft, has not said, 'You've snatched at the end again, darling.'

It is a temptation. You know that you have said all that you have to say in your book. You have, if it is that sort of book, exposed your murderer and accounted for the way the murder was committed. You have subtly put before your readers enough of what it was you felt you had to say about this complicated business called life. So you come to a halt.

But in all probability you have forgotten one thing, something I mentioned when talking about the classical detective story. Form. To give the reader that satisfied feeling that comes from the completion of a promised form you have to round off your book in a way that readers will, not necessarily recognise, but feel on their pulses. You should aim for an effect similar to that of the final bars of a symphony. Hearing those, you as a listener know that this is the conclusion, that the work is finished.

So you should write your last pages with that thought firmly in mind. Probably this alone will be enough. The words you use, the cadences you put them into, will then say to your readers, 'Amen'. Yet quite often there will be no need for the full solemnity of an amen. Sometimes it will be enough to sign off thoroughly by, say, writing a paragraph that says 'The End' and then adding a little final-final note in the form of a joke. For a book that has not been too weighty in tone this will be the right treatment. Erle Stanley Gardner, for instance, invariably used the pay-off joke in his Perry Mason books, where it was just what was needed.

Since the book you will be writing will be crime fiction, that is entertainment fiction, your ending will also need to be a happy one. But, of course, it does not need to be the plain, full-out happy ending of a romantic film (not even if you are writing a romantic suspense novel). An ending is happy when it shows that justice has been done and has been seen to be done. The final words often used by one of the great producers of Golden Age detective stories, John Rhode (no particular need, really, to read him), 'And he was duly hanged' are, in fact, a happy ending.

Indeed, if you are working on a book of as much subtlety as the crime novel your happy ending may well be largely on a downbeat note. But, since you are writing not a novel but a crime novel, you should have some small upward twist to that down beat. A few words from another cutting loose in my notebook are from an interview with the film director, Francois Truffaut. He makes the point that a film (like crime fiction) is entertainment. 'In a film' he says, 'the director gives the audience a promise of pleasure.' But, he goes on to say that the curve of life is not pleasure promising. It goes, he says with Gallic realism, towards decadence, decrepitude, illness and extinction. But in a film he wants a rising curve. 'One achieves this by a manipulation of elements.' He makes the very last moments of his films say, 'Happy'. And so should you with your books.

One way you can manipulate the down-drooping curve of life is by leaving things unsaid, by leaving the reader with the feeling that your people will go on living after they have reached your last page. There is no need to make a meal of this. A hint or two will do, and you will find hints come tapping off the keys of your word-processor if you simply think hard enough of these people living on afterwards. Perhaps a somewhat enigmatic sentence of Raymond Chandler's will give you an insight about what to aim at. 'The ideal mystery,' he once said, 'is one you would read if the end was missing.' An element of exaggeration there, I think, though I am sometimes tempted to write a book actually without an ending, perhaps just sticking this quotation on the last page. But I doubt if I could get it past a publisher.

The writing life

Before we end this look at the actual writing of one of the forms of crime fiction we examined earlier, let me share with you some of the hints I have picked up over the years about how to get that writing done.

And the first thing to say is: write. I myself, I must admit, have not had any difficulty over this. Even in the short period of my life when I thought I wasn't going to be a writer (by which I mean a writer of fiction) I constantly found reasons to be writing something. But I know a good many writers who once had difficulty getting going, and their advice has been consistent. Write. Set aside some time every day if you possibly can and write something. The mere doing of it will, first, lead perhaps to something worthwhile or, at worst, will improve your skills.

Then don't be put off if at the beginning of what you are writing, you find it's painfully slow work. The start of any book is likely to be slow going. Although you may have thought about it long and hard, turned the gas up high under the porridge pot, stirred much and often, it is still only when you are actually creating that the unconscious mind is fully engaged, and until you have advanced some way into your book it is likely that the under-mind does not have as much as it might to work with.

One way of overcoming this obstacle which suits certain writers, though not me at all, is to write first some part of a book that they know they are going to need and which passionately interests them. If you adopt their method, you may have to make adjustments to this section later but if doing it has got the juices flowing up from the unconscious it will have been worthwhile.

Let me add another tip, seemingly crude. Set yourself a deadline. One day maybe it will be a clause in a contract for your next book specifying the date it should be delivered. But it need not be anything as legalistic. (Most publishers know darn well they will be lucky to get that mss on time.) It can be simply 'Christmas'; or the start of a holiday six or eight months away; anything. But, crude and ridiculous even though the idea is, it actually works. It forces the mind to do that immensely difficult thing, create a little world that has never existed.

Something now about the way of creating that world. First, about what it consists of. I have said it is a little world that has never existed, and the consequence of this, if you think about it, is that its 'facts' are not going to be the facts of the world that does exist.

Of course, some of them are. When I was leaving the army
in 1947 all conscripts were offered courses designed to fit
them for civilian life. The course I chose was on writing,
though I don't think I imagined that it was going to make me
into a writer earning a living in just four weeks. But one of the
exercises we were given to do was to write a story in which
two and two did not make four. (Perhaps I'm making this up;
1947 was a long time ago.) None of us on the course got very
far with it. It's an impossibility. Some facts from the real world
do have to form part of the unreal world you are creating.

But by no means every fact does. And it is by no means
easy to accustom oneself to realising this. Take an example
from the crime world. You have invented a murder and a
dead body. All right, you are apt to say, what will happen
next? Oh, yes, the police will come along. And who will they
be? Ah, yes, something called 'The Team'. I must find out just
who they would be. Well, you must not. Or not unless you are
writing a police procedural, and perhaps not even then. What
you should have asked yourself as soon as you had invented
that dead body was: what will the reader want to know next?
And for your sort of story this might be something very different from the police arriving at the scene.

What you need is not, then, facts, the facts of the real world,
but something I have briefly mentioned already, the things
I call fiction-facts. These are such facts and only such facts—
they will be a mixture of real-world facts and 'facts' you may
have totally invented—as are needed for the story you are
telling. They will be what create your little world, reflecting
the real world distantly but not directly stemming from it.

Facts from the real world that you don't need for your
fiction serve only to clog things up, to slow down your story,
to take away from the vividness of your descriptions, to
obfuscate the characters you are drawing. So, to descend
to practicalities, you should perhaps impose on yourself a
deliberate limit of, say, half a page, some 150 words, for any
description of a place. And ten lines at most for the description of a face, with every 'fact' being one that will glow in the
reader's mind. I know the great novelists of the past gave
themselves much more scope than the limits I have suggested, but they were great novelists, men and women
writing at high intensity, and that carried them through. For
us lesser mortals, less ambition.

What carried these great ones through, what the actual

manifestation of their intensity was, was words. They had the gift of using the exact word, and no more (though, of course, the gift could desert them). And this is the aim we, too, should have in our minds. A high, high aim, but the best. Each time one uses a word that is not the best possible one it probably does almost nothing to take away from the vivid, mind-impressing book we might have written. But repeat those tiny inaccuracies and sooner or later the whole becomes fuzzed.

Christianna Brand, author of that classic detective story *Green for Danger* (read it) had an analogy for this which I have found makes it stick in my head. Talking to would-be writers she would take off her spectacles and lay them on the table in front of her, lenses down. That, she would say, will have made only the tiniest scratch on them, something virtually invisible. But do this time and again and before you know it when you put the specs back on you will be looking through a thick blur.

It is a difficult thing we are doing, using just the right word, creating a world, however small, that doesn't exist. There are some people, lucky people, who do this without strain. But for most of us it is hard. Simenon after just one hour at his typewriter always had to change his shirt, so sweat-soaked had it become.

And, damn it, we have to start every day anew. It is as if, to go back to my feeling of being on the high diving-board at the start of a book, that we have to go up at least to the middle board time and again during our swim. So a tip or two on making it easier. Some clearing of the mind between going to one's work and actually beginning is a good thing. I myself read the newspaper in as desultory a fashion as possible, paying more attention to the lists of TV shows' popularity than to the earnest leaders or the Page One splash. But I suspect I would do better, if I ever could get round to it, to use some yoga or meditation. Empty the mind, that's the object.

Then another clever wrinkle is to take care to leave off the day before (and no matter how short your stint you should try and do something every day) at a point where you know well what you want to say next. Always leave it pointing downhill, Hemingway once said. Occasionally I have left a sentence deliberately unfinished, though I have not always found next day that I knew how I had intended to go on. However, leaving off in mid-flow was the sole piece of advice Graham Greene offered Sir Alec Guinness when he heard he was contemplating a book.

And, something else I adopted from Graham Greene: at night take what you have written to bed with you and read it over last thing. Partly, this sends stuff down to the subconscious, and partly it prepares you for the next day's task. It is I think, a good idea too, to read over the day-before's words before starting new writing.

You will, no doubt, find yourself then reaching for the keys of your word processor or for your pencil and making revisions. Well and good. You can hardly revise too much, There is a charming and humble saying of the Indian novelist, R. K. Narayan. He said on television once that increasingly over the years he spends longer and longer revising—'to make it worthy of being printed'. Now, when your story has reached its end, you must subdue the creator in you and bring forward, as much as you can, the critic, 'to make it worthy of being printed'. Sophia Tolstoy complained, in her diary for June 18, 1887, of the great Lev Nikolayevich that 'no sooner am I finished copying than he changes it all, and I have to copy it all over again. His patience and determination are endless.'

There is still time to replace the inexact word with the one that is exactly right. It takes time. You may think that for a few tiny alterations it isn't worth it. I believe it is. It is in the tiny things that the difference lies between a book that's all right and a book that the reader will remember, or between perhaps a book that a publisher turns down, just, and a book that he is delighted to publish.

So revise slowly and with the utmost care. It's tough advice, and I fail myself sometimes to apply it with total rigour. The old creator creeps back and I read as if I was living in the world I have made again. But I try and stop myself. I intend to look at every adjective and ask if it needs to be there, and with yet more suspicion, I look at every adverb. 'Go away,' he said mulishly. Is that 'mulishly' implied from the context? If it is, out it comes.

Then when I have gone over the book for the words and gone over it separately for the logic of the whole, adding some passages to make things clearer, cutting others that are unnecessary, I read the whole aloud. Graham Greene again, from a TV interview I think, 'I'm a great reader-alouder.' Failure to do this, he thought, was what made some authors hard to read.

So now at last has everything been done? Well, there's

always the title to type on the title page. Sometimes you may have thought of a title right from the start. Sometimes, indeed, it is a title that flashes into the mind and 'says' the whole book to the author. And no bad thing. One ought to be able to say in a phrase at least, if not in one word, what the book is about, what its theme is. And if hitting on a title helps one to do this, that's fine. Seeing that title day in and day out as you work means that the fundamental drive of the book will stay all the more firmly in your mind, and it is this that gives the underlying power.

But what if no title has come into the mind, floating up from the subconscious? There have been occasions when I have had two whole pages of my notebook scrawled with possible titles, perhaps as many as thirty of them. What makes a good one? It is important, ridiculous but important, to have as good a title as you can. If only to make your book stand out a little among the 250 or more crime books that as a reviewer used to come on to my desk each year.

So, another admonition I once wrote to myself in my writer's notebook: 'The ordinary "good" title is too much like all the other good titles, the fragment of a quotation or the neat alliteration. What is wanted is an unusual juxtaposition of words with marked echoic qualities. You could even write a poem about your book and use one line. A title is a poem, indeed.' And, to complicate this even more, you may as a writer of crime fiction have to indicate to your future readers that you have entered into the unwritten contract with them by getting in one of those key words, 'Dead' or 'Death' or 'Crime' or 'Inspector' or what have you.

But when you have found your title and typed it on that title page you may say to yourself that at last your task is over. After this, it will be in the lap of the gods.

6
Last Words

There remains something to say about the technicalities of getting your crime fiction published.

To begin with, what should the actual stuff you send to a publisher look like? First of all, it must of course be typed, or printed from a word-processor, and in double spacing. If you type yourself, take pains to be neat (alas, a messy typescript does put publishers' editors off), and above all be accurate. Use A4 paper, which is a standard size that helps publishers estimate the length of your book. Change the machine's ribbon if it's getting feeble. Make a copy, so that in the rare event of your typescript getting lost at the publisher's or in the post you are still in the game. Number your pages. Keep a decent margin, partly so that editors can make notes and corrections eventually, partly because of the amount of photocopying that goes on nowadays which might mean bits of your deathless words disappearing off the duplicated page.

Put, of course, your name and address on the title page together with the approximate number of words, and it is a good idea to repeat name and address on the last page as well. Bind the whole up securely, though not so securely that the pages cannot be turned. Many publishers, however, welcome from a first novelist not the whole typescript but just the first couple of chapters and a synopsis. And make that synopsis as short as you can. Write out for yourself, if it helps, a full account of the book with all the clever bits there. But for the busy editor or agent (one of the latter told me recently, she gets 100 submissions a week) keep it to one side of one sheet only.

Then send off either your sample or your whole manuscript, with a stamped and addressed envelope or label for reply. But to whom?

The best answer is for you to get it clear in your mind once again just what sort of a crime fiction book you have written and then to visit a library or large bookshop and see which publishers have, within the last year or two, published something similar to your own book. Almost all the major publishers, however, produce at least some crime fiction, and some of them produce a fair amount. There are also a good many small publishing firms that will take an occasional crime book. Paperback houses in Britain on the whole do not, of course, publish original fiction, though there are some who do, particularly crime and science fiction.

Then when your darling has been entrusted to the post (and if you're especially anxious you can enclose a stamped and addressed acknowledgement card), what happens? Silence happens.

Publishers get hundreds of manuscripts. They have only so many people to read them. So it does take a long time for a first novel to get looked at. You should allow three whole months. Then if you have heard nothing you can feel entitled to write and ask what's up.

Don't call at the offices personally, not even with a horse-whip. It is quite possible that at that moment your book will be in the hands of one of the outside readers most publishing firms employ, people who have become experts by experience at assessing the potential of submitted manuscripts. One of them, Christopher Derrick, (who read at least one of my novels for a publisher, and commented on it partly in Latin) has written a book about his experiences, *Reader's Report*. You may find things in it that are helpful.

But the photocopier has created a small revolution in the publishing world, going under the name of 'multiple submission'. You can have run off as many copies of your typescript as you can afford and you can send them off simultaneously to a number of firms. Opinions vary about the ethics of this. One publisher I have heard of instantly rejects any book he believes to be a multiple submission. Others say they feel they ought to be told. Yet others are quite content to receive books in this way. I leave it to you.

One way of avoiding the dilemma is to send your book not to a publisher but to a literary agent. This, if you can find an agent who will take you on, is something that has a good many advantages. Publishers, again, vary in what they say about books submitted to them by agents. Some claim they receive no better treatment; most admit they look on agented authors with a kindlier eye. Certainly, if you can get an agent, you are unlikely to have to wait as long as those three months for a publisher's verdict.

Then, too, an agent will know better than you where to send your book. He may have heard on the grapevine, for instance, that Messrs So-and-so still have a hole in their Spring list for a good crime story. And an agent will know, as well, what are the going rates and may be able to get you something a little above them, probably enough to cancel out the ten per cent commission charged.

In addition an agent will be able to secure you good terms in all the many subsidiary rights that can accrue from book publication, not only American rights and other foreign ones and paperback rights, but such obscure, but not altogether to be sneezed at, things as excerpts read on the radio. Publishers, though nice people, are seldom above presenting a new author with what they call their standard contract, which is often quite heavily loaded in favour of themselves.

But it is not altogether easy to get an agent. If your book is a clear bestseller you will have no difficulty. If it's just good and perfectly publishable you are in danger of finding that many of the agents you approach have all the authors they can handle.

Where to find those mysterious and useful figures? The answer is the *Writers' & Artists' Yearbook*, which not only lists agents by the dozen but also prints their mini-prospectuses, some of which say specifically 'New and established authors'. I recommend you to become well acquainted with the *Writers' & Artists' Yearbook*. It gives you the addresses of publishers and agents as well as containing a section of good advice for would-be authors.

I have in the course of writing recommended a good many books, both as examples and as aids, and I think there is only one more I should add. This is a book called *Dear Author*, written by Michael Legat, gamewarden turned poacher, i.e., a former senior publisher in both paperback and hardback fields who is now an author. It contains much extremely sensible information.

Advice and support can also be obtained from the various societies that cater for authors, though most of these, in the nature of things, cater for published authors. But there are the numerous writers groups scattered round the country and joining one of these can be decidedly helpful. Not only will you often get useful advice and criticism from the members of your trial efforts, but you will be in the company of others doing what you are doing and there's much comfort in that. Your local library will probably have an address.

When you do have something accepted by a regular publisher, or even a short story or two read perhaps on BBC radio, you will be eligible to join the Crime Writers Association (address in the *Writers' & Artists'*). This organisation, founded by the multi-pseudonymed John Creasey, holds monthly meetings in London at some of which expert speakers are to be heard, as well as yearly meetings in various parts of the country. It also has a mini-library of pamphlets which members can buy, on various subjects such as guns and poisons, and it issues a monthly newsletter which generally contains a good deal of interest to both new and old crime writers.

Then there are, for all authors, two organisations. The Society of Authors, which publishes *The Author*, a journal that always has material of interest, even vitally, to authors, and an advice department second to none in the world. You can have your contracts vetted (even your first one) by experts and, if you chance to fall into some legal or financial trap, you can get weighty backing. Writers who have had even the occasional article published can join as associate members. Or there is the Writers' Guild, especially good for television and film writers, but also serving book writers. The addresses are to be found, guess where, in the *Writers' & Artists' Yearbook*.

So I come to my final piece of advice. And that is simply this: if you want to become a published author of crime fiction, read as much as you can of what the established authors have written. Don't be afraid that you will pick up the style of a Raymond Chandler or an Agatha Christie. If you read plentifully you will be in no danger of that. Instead, invisibly as it were, by reacting favourably to some sentences or turns of expression and less favourably to others you will gradually acquire a style of your own, stamped in the deepest recesses of your mind. (This tip, courtesy of the great American, Mark Twain.) You will also see what has been done, and be in less danger of spending long hours and weeks producing what has already saturated the market. And from what others have done you will gain inspiration to do something the same, only different, yourself.

Good luck.

Books Recommended

Barnard, Robert *A Scandal in Belgravia*
Berkeley, Anthony *The Second Shot*
Braine, John *Writing a Novel*
Brand, Christianna *Green for Danger*
Carr, John Dickson *Bride of Newgate*
  Devil in Velvet
  The Hollow Man
Christie, Agatha *An Autobiography*
  Death Comes as the End
  Death on the Nile
  One, Two, Buckle my Shoe
  The Mysterious Affair at Styles
Collins, Wilkie *The Moonstone*
Davie, Donald *The Heyday of Sir Walter Scott*
Derrick, Christopher *Reader's Report*
Ellin, Stanley *The Speciality of the House*
Forster, E.M. *Aspects of a Novel*
Freeman, Austin R. *The Singing Bone*
Hammett, Dashiell *The Maltese Falcon*
Highsmith, Patricia *Strangers on a Train*
Iles, Francis *Before the Fact*
  Malice Aforethought
James, P.D. *Unnatural Causes*
Keating, H.R.F. *Death and the Visiting Firemen*
  Go West, Inspector Ghote
  Inspector Ghote Draws a Line
  Inspector Ghote Trusts the Heart
  The Murder of the Maharajah
  The Perfect Murder
  Zen There was Murder
Legat, Michael *An Author's Guide to Publishing*
  Dear Author
Malone, Michael *Handling Sin*
Maurier, Daphne Du *The Rebecca Notebook*
Mitchell, Gladys *Late, Late in the Evening*
Orwell, George *The Decline of the English Murder*

Poe, Edgar Allan *The Murders in the Rue Morgue*
  The Mystery of Marie Roget
  The Purloined Letter
Quennell, Marjorie and B. *History of Everyday Things in England*
Rendell, Ruth *Born Victim*
Rinehart, Mary Roberts *The Circular Staircase*
Sayers, Dorothy L. *Five Red Herrings*
  Murder Must Advertise
  The Nine Tailors
  Whose Body?
Simenon, Georges *Maigret's Pickpocket*
Symons, Julian *As If By Magic*
  The Man Who Lost His Wife
Tey, Josephine *The Daughters of Time*
Thomson, June *A Question of Identity*
Treat, Lawrence *V as Victim*
Waugh, Hillary *Last Seen Wearing*
Writers' & Artists' Yearbook

Index

A Child of the Jago 79
A Rush on the Ultimate 87
An Autobiography 20, 36
action scenes 38, 71
agents 106
angel-over-the-shoulder 11
Aiken, Joan vii
Allingham, Margery 7, 10, 94
'Angel' 62
'Appleby, Sir John' 59
'Archer' 46
As If by Magic 22
Aspects of the Novel 90
Aubrey Fletcher, Henry 49
Austen, Jane 34
Author, The 108

backgrounder 28
Barnard, Robert 76
Barnes, Linda 48
Beerbohm, Max 76
Before the Fact 27
'Bennet, Elizabeth' 56
Berkeley, Anthony 27
Black Mask 43
Blake, Nicholas 17
Born Victim 80, 83
Braine, John 95, 97
Brand, Christianna 102
'Brandstetter, Dave' 44, 60
Brontë Sisters 65
'Brown, Father' 79
Bunyan, John 87, 88

'Campion, Mr' 10
'Carlyle, Carlotta' 48
Carr, John Dickson 13, 17, 21
Castle of Otranto, The 65
Chandler, Raymond 16, 23, 43,
   45, 60, 99, 108
Chase, James Hadley 44
chase scenes 71
characters 87
Chesterton, G.K. 9, 79
Christie, Agatha 8, 9, 11, 14, 15,
   19, 20, 23, 24, 28, 32, 36, 37,
   46, 61, 73, 87, 88, 108
Circular Staircase, The 66, 70
Clifford, Francis 58
'Clouseau Inspector' 62
clues 11, 91
Cody, Liza 44, 45, 48
Collins, Wilkie 5
comic crime 59
Copper, Basil 44
Conrad, Joseph 88
Creasey, John 49, 52, 53, 54,
   108
'Cribb, Sergeant' 73
Crime and Punishment 40
crime novels 39
Crippen, Dr 6
Curtiss, Ursula 57

'Dalgleish, Commander' 39
'Darcy' 56
Daughter of Time, The 77

Davie, Professor Donald 35, 90
Davis, Lindsay 73
Dear Author 107
Death and the Visiting Firemen 8
Death Comes As the End 73
Death on the Nile 15
Decline of the English Murder, The 77
Derrick, Christopher 106
detective novels 34
Dostoievsky 40, 41
'Dover, Inspector' 63
Doyle, Conan 9, 10, 79, 88
'Duffy' 44
Du Maurier, Daphne 84
'Duncan, King' 60
'Dupin' 8, 9, 10

Eden, Dorothy 69
Egan, Leslie 54
Eliot, T.S. 4
Ellery Queen's Mystery Magazine 82, 84
Ellin, Stanley 80, 83, 84
explanations 96

'Faraday, Mike' 44
farce crime 63
'Fell, Dr' 13
female private-eye novels 47
Ferrars, Elizabeth 33
fiction-facts 68, 100
'Finch, Inspector' 15
finishing 98
Five Red Herrings, The 12, 29
Flypaper War, The 95
form 22, 23, 98
Forster, E.M. 90
Francis, Dick 57, 86, 94
Freeman, R. Austin 26, 96
Fremlin, Celia 57
Freud, Sigmund 20
Futrelle, Jacques 79

Gardner, Erle Stanley 98
'Ghote, Inspector' 9, 18, 37, 62–3, 67, 92, 93, 97
'Gideon, Commander' 49, 52, 53
Gilbert, Michael 51
Gill, Anton 73
gothic novels 65
Go West, Inspector Ghote 21
Governess, The 72
Grafton, Sue 48
Great Detective, the 8, 44, 51, 79
Green for Danger 102
Greene, Graham 36, 38, 71, 72, 94, 102, 103
Guinness, Sir Alec 102

Hammett, Dashiell 43, 46, 47
Handling Sin 61
Hansen, Joseph 44, 60
'Hastings, Captain' 11
Hemingway, Ernest 102
hermeneutic error 18
Hervey, Evelyn 8, 72
'Hewitt, Martin' 79
Heyday of Sir Walter Scott, The 35
Hiassen, Carl 61
Highsmith, Patricia 17, 58
History of Everyday Things in England 74
Hitchcock, Alfred 93
Hole in the Wall, The 79
Hollow Man, The 21
'Holmes, Sherlock' 8, 9, 10, 27, 54, 79
how-dun-its 31

Iles, Francis 27
Innes, Michael 59
'Innes, Rachel' 66
Inspector Ghote Draws A Line 20, 37

Inspector Ghote Trusts the Heart 86
interviews 95
inverted stories 26
Ison, Graham 49

Jane Eyre 65
James, P.D. vii, 4, 7, 11, 16, 19, 35, 39
Jonson, Ben 7

Kavanagh, Dan 44
Kent, Constance 77

Lacey, Sarah 48
Last Seen Wearing 49
Le Carré, John 4
Legat, Michael 107
'Lee, Anna' 44, 45
Lewis, Cecil Day 17
Linington, Elizabeth 54
locked-room stories 21
Lonely Magdalen, The 49
looking-back novels 76
Lovesey, Peter 73

MacAdoo, Thomas Ozro 22, 47
McBain, Ed 49
Macbeth 59, 60
Macdonald, Gregory 89
'Maigret' 19, 36, 52
Maigret's Pickpocket 19, 52
Maclean, Alastair 38
Malice Aforethought 27
Malone, Michael 61
Malory 45
Maltese Falcon, The 46
'Mason, Perry' 98
Man Who Lost His Wife, The 61
'Marple, Miss' 8, 47
Marsh, Ngaio 23
Marric, J.J. 49
Maupassant, Guy de 80, 84

Masterman, Sir John 7, 26
Melville, Jennie 67
Millar, Margaret 57
'Milverton, Charles Augustus' 88
Moliére 53
Moonstone, The 5
'Moriarty, Professor' 88
Morrison, Arthur 79
motives 6
multiple submission 106
Murders in the Rue Morgue, The 10, 21
Murder of the Maharajah, The 13, 19
Murder Must Advertise 29
Murdoch, Iris 38
Mysterious Affairs at Styles, The 87
Mystery of Marie Roget, The 10
mystery with history 72

names 88
Narayan, R.K. 103
Nash, Ogden 70
Nine Tailors, The 11, 29
Norden, Denis 95
notebooks 89

One, Two, Buckle My Shoe 11
Orwell, George 77

Paretsky, Sara 48
Paris Review 93
Parker, Robert B. 44, 45
pastiche 73
Perfect Murder, The 18, 21, 30
plagiarism 53
planting 90
plot 90
police procedurals 48
Poe, Edgar Allan 8, 9, 10, 15, 21, 48, 51

'Poirot Hercule' 11, 15, 36, 93
Porte, Joyce 63
private-eye novels 43
Purloined Letter, The 10
'Purbright, Inspector' 64

Question of Identity, A 15
Queen, Ellery 43
Quennell, M. and D.H.B. 74

Reader's Report 106
real crime into fiction 77
Rebecca Notebook, The 84
Rendell, Ruth vii, 39, 53, 80, 83, 84
Renoir, Jean 88
revision 103
Rhode, John 99
riddles 91
Rinehart, Mary Roberts 66, 70
Ripley, Mike 62
'Ripley, Tom' 58
romantic suspense 65
'Roylott, Grimesby' 88
Runyon, Damon 2

Sandoe, James 45
Sayers, Dorothy L. 9, 10, 11, 12, 13, 16, 28, 82
'Scarlet Pimpernel, The' 10
Scandal in Belgravia, A 76
scenes 93
Second Shot, The 27
second murder, the 24
Sellers, Peter 62
Shannon, Dell 54
Shakespeare 60
short stories 78
Simenon, Georges 19, 36, 52, 102
Singing Bone, The 26
Society of Authors 108
'Spade, Sam' 46

Speciality of the House, The 80
'Spenser' 44, 45
Starnes, Richard 95
stock responses 13
storyline 23, 72
Stout, Rex 43
Strangers on a Train 17
surprises and shocks 94
suspects 5
suspense 55
switch-point, the 16
Symons, Julian 22, 41, 61

Tey, Josephine 77
Thomson, June 14
'Thorndyke, Dr' 27
time 96, 97
titles 104
Tolstoy, Lev Nikolayevich 103
Tolstoy, Sophia 103
Treat, Lawrence 49
Trollope, Anthony 97
Truffaut, Francois 99
Twohy, Robert 84

Unnatural Causes 16
'Unwin, Miss' 72
Updike, John 93

V As in Victim 49
'Van Dusen, Professor' 79

Wade, Henry 48
Wainwright, John 49, 50
Walpole, Horace 65
Wallace, Edgar 6, 77
Watson, Colin 63–4
'Watson, Dr' 9, 10, 11, 27, 54
Waugh, Hillary 49
Westlake, Donald E. 64, 83
Welty, Eudora 24, 41
Whose Body? 16
why-dun-its 31

'Wimsey, Lord Peter' 10, 29
Writing A Novel 95
writing life, the 99
Writers' & Artists' Yearbook 107, 108
Writers' Guild 108

Wright, Keith 49
Wuthering Heights 65

Yorke, Margaret vii

Zen There Was Murder 18